Frommer's™

Vienna
day BY day™

1st Edition

by Teresa Fisher

WILEY
A John Wiley and Sons, Ltd, Publication

Contents

Explore over 3,500 destinations.

Frommers.com makes it easy.

Find a destination. ✓ Book a trip. ✓ Get hot travel deals.
Buy a guidebook. ✓ Enter to win vacations. ✓ Listen to podcasts.
Check out the latest travel news. ✓ Share trip photos and memories.
And much more.

day BY day

Get the best of a city in 1, 2 or 3 days

Day by Day Destinations

Europe

Amsterdam
Athens
Barcelona
Berlin
Bordeaux &
  Southwest France
Brussels & Bruges
Budapest
Edinburgh
Dublin
Florence and Tuscany
Lisbon
London
Madrid
Malta & Gozo
Moscow
Paris
Provence & the Riviera

Prague
Rome
Seville
St Petersburg
Stockholm
Valencia
Vienna
Venice

Canada and The Americas

Boston
Cancun & the Yucatan
Chicago
Honolulu & Oahu

Los Angeles
Las Vegas
Maui
Montreal
Napa & Sonama
New York City
San Diego
San Francisco
Seattle
Washington

Rest of the World

Beijing
Hong Kong

UK Publisher: Sally Smith
Executive Project Editor: Daniel Mersey
Commissioning Editor: Mark Henshall
Development Editor: Lindsay Hunt
Project Editor: Hannah Clement
Photo Research: Jill Emeny
Cartographer: Tim Lohnes

Wiley also publishes its books in a variety of electronic formats. Some
content that appears in print may not be available in electronic books.

British Library Cataloguing in Publication Data

A catalogue record for this book is available from the British Library

ISBN: 978-0-470-71556-7

Typeset by Wiley Indianapolis Composition Services

Printed and bound in China by RR Donnelley

5 4 3 2 1

A Note from the Editorial Director

Organizing your time. That's what this guide is all about.

Other guides give you long lists of things to see and do and then expect you to fit the pieces together. The Day by Day guides are different. These guides tell you the best of everything, and then they show you how to see it *in the smartest, most time-efficient way*. Our authors have designed detailed itineraries organized by time, neighborhood, or special interest. And each tour comes with a bulleted map that takes you from stop to stop.

Would you like to wind back the clock to Imperial times at the Hofburg, visit Mozart's house, cruise the Blue Danube or admire Lipizzaner horses strutting to Waltz music? Or catch a tram along epic Viennesse boulevards and visit the Prater ferris wheel of Vienna's cult movie, *The Third Man*? Hoping to sample some of Viennese legendary coffee houses or snack on a large Wiener schnitzel? Whatever your interest or schedule, the Day by Days give you the smartest routes to follow. Not only do we take you to the top attractions, hotels, and restaurants, but we also help you access those special moments that locals get to experience—those "finds" that turn tourists into travelers.

The Day by Days are also your top choice if you're looking for one complete guide for all your travel needs. The best hotels and restaurants for every budget, the greatest shopping values, the wildest nightlife—it's all here.

Why should you trust our judgment? Because our authors personally visit each place they write about. They're an independent lot who say what they think and would never include places they wouldn't recommend to their best friends. They're also open to suggestions from readers. If you'd like to contact them, please send your comments our way at feedback@frommers.com, and we'll pass them on.

Enjoy your Day by Day guide—the most helpful travel companion you can buy. And have the trip of a lifetime.

Warm regards,

Kelly Regan

Kelly Regan, Editorial Director
Frommer's Travel Guides

About the Author

Freelance travel writer and photographer **Teresa Fisher** has been a regular visitor to Vienna for over 25 years, lured by the art and architecture, the coffee houses and especially the city's rich musical heritage. Although this is her first book for Frommer's, she has authored more than twenty guidebooks for a variety of publishers (including Thomas Cook, Lonely Planet and the AA). A fluent German speaker, a music graduate and a specialist in European city breaks, Teresa was the obvious choice to write *Vienna Day by Day*.

Acknowledgments

To Angelika Grzebyta and Margot Neugebauer at WienTourismus for patiently answering my endless queries; to my two sons, George and Timothy, for showing me how child-friendly and fun the city is by day, and to Carl for baby-sitting by night; and finally to Mark, Jill and Hannah at Frommer's for all their support and help.

An Additional Note

Please be advised that travel information is subject to change at any time—and this is especially true of prices. We therefore suggest that you write or call ahead for confirmation when making your travel plans. The authors, editors, and publisher cannot be held responsible for the experiences of readers while traveling. Your safety is important to us, however, so we encourage you to stay alert and be aware of your surroundings.

Star Ratings, Icons & Abbreviations

Every hotel, restaurant, and attraction listing in this guide has been ranked for quality, value, service, amenities, and special features using a **star-rating system.** Hotels, restaurants, attractions, shopping, and nightlife are rated on a scale of zero stars (recommended) to three stars (exceptional). In addition to the star-rating system, we also use a **kids icon** to point out the best bets for families. Within each tour, we recommend cafes, bars or restaurants where you can take a break. Each of these stops appears in a shaded box marked with a coffee cup–shaped bullet 🍵 .

The following **abbreviations** are used for credit cards:

AE American Express	DISC Discover	V Visa
DC Diners Club	MC MasterCard	

Frommers.com

Now that you have this guidebook to help you plan a great trip, visit our website at **www.frommers.com** for additional travel information on more than 4,000 destinations. We update features regularly to give you instant access to the most current trip-planning information available. At Frommers. com, you'll find scoops on the best airfares, lodging rates, and car rental bargains. You can even book your travel online through our reliable travel booking partners. Other popular features include:

A Note on Prices

In the "Take a Break" and "Best Bets" sections of this book, we have used a system of dollar signs to show a range of costs for 1 night in a hotel (the price of a double-occupancy room) or the cost of an entree (main meal) at a restaurant. Use the following table to decipher the dollar signs:

Cost	Hotels	Restaurants
$	under $100	under $10
$$	$100–$200	$10–$20
$$$	$200–$300	$20–$30
$$$$	$300–$400	$30–$40
$$$$$	over $400	over $40

An Invitation to the Reader

In researching this book, we discovered many wonderful places—hotels, restaurants, shops, and more. We're sure you'll find others. Please tell us about them, so we can share the information with your fellow travelers in upcoming editions. If you were disappointed with a recommendation, we'd love to know that, too. Please write to:

Frommer's Vienna Day by Day, 1st Edition
Wiley Publishing, Inc. • 111 River St. • Hoboken, NJ 07030-577

14 Favorite
Moments

14 Favorite Moments

1. Spanish Riding School
2. Café Sperl
3. Hofburg
4. Figlmüller
5. Prater ferris wheel
6. Graben (a), Kohlmarkt (b),
   Kärntnerstrasse (c),
   MAK (d), Naschmarkt (e)
7. Grinzing
8. Café Sacher
9. Ringstrasse
10. Christmas market
    at Rathaus-Platz
11. Schönbrunn Palace
12. Gürtel
13. Danube
14. Musikverein

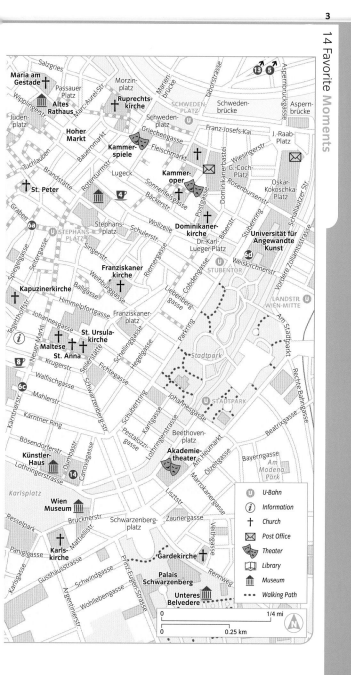

Like a catchy waltz tune, Vienna makes my heart beat faster. Much more than Mozart and museums, this stately city is constantly reinventing itself. Modern art and vibrant nightlife are as much part of the Vienna of today as the grand concert halls and baroque architecture of its imperial heyday. Amid the pomp and splendor of its stately parks and palaces drifts an air of romance and easy living—a seductive charm at once relaxing yet compelling.

1 Admire the discipline and control of the Spanish Riding School, as meticulously schooled Lipizzaner horses strut and pirouette to waltz music. Nothing can match a full performance, but if you can't get tickets, watch the informal morning exercises instead. Not all the classic moves, such as the *croupade*, the *levade*, or the *capriole*, are practiced every day, but, if you're lucky, you should certainly witness some startling equine ballet. *See p 44, bullet* **5**.

2 Crack the code of the coffee menu at one of the city's legendary Kaffeehäuser. Viennese coffee houses range from basic, boho and nicotine-stained to the sophisticated *fin-de-siècle* grandeur of my favorite, Café Sperl. Many have long literary associations. Coffee-drinking is virtually an art form in Vienna: choose a *Melange* (coffee

Vienna's vineyards are just a short tram ride away.

with frothy milk); a *kleiner* or *grosser Brauner* (large or small coffee with cream); an *Einspänner* (mocha with whipped cream); a *Fiaker* (mocha

Kids large and small love to ride the Riesenrad.

with brandy)… the list goes on. *See The Best Dining, p 109.*

❸ Wind back the clocks to imperial times at the Hofburg and see how the 19th-century Habsburg Empress Sisi, darling of Viennese society, lived in these grandiose palace apartments. Discover how all that glittered was not gold for Vienna's own 'Princess Diana' figure, whose tragic life came to an abrupt end in 1898. *See p 29, bullet* ❺.

❹ Tuck into the largest Wiener schnitzel in the world at Figlmüller. This tiny, *pseudo-rustique* restaurant is always crowded and a bit touristy. But who cares when the legendary schnitzels are so big that they overlap the plates? They taste pretty good too, washed down with a *G'spritzer* (white wine spritzer). Be prepared to queue. *See p 10, bullet* ❷.

❺ Take photos from the top of the Prater ferris wheel. Aerial views of the city and the Vienna Woods beyond are especially enticing at sunset, when the city glows in mellow evening light and lamps begin to twinkle. You can also relive the key scene in Vienna's cult movie, *The Third Man,* when the two anti-heroes finally meet on the wheel. *See p 98, bullet* ❹.

❻ Indulge in some serious retail therapy in the shops of Graben, Kohlmarkt, and Kärntnerstrasse. Take the pulse of the city's young fashion designers in the trendy Neubau district; gather home-furnishing ideas at the MAK (the Museum of Applied Arts) boutique; then shop for a picnic at the bustling Naschmarkt, where the photogenic food stalls are a feast for the senses. *See The Best Shopping, p 79.*

❼ Stroll through the Vienna Woods and taste some local wines. Few of the world's capitals grow wine within the city limits. A visit to some of the cozy *Heurigen*

Tour the Ringstrasse on tram 1 or 2.

(wine taverns) in the romantic wine-growing villages on Vienna's outskirts always makes an enjoyable excursion. Take your camera to capture stunning views over Vienna from the vine-striped hills. *See The Great Outdoors, p 93.*

❽ Forget the calories and enjoy "Kuchen mit Schlag" at Café Sacher. Vienna is cake-and-whipped-cream heaven. It's hard to stick to the straight and narrow when confronted by a formidable choice of gooey gâteaux. Some of my favorite cakes are the ones called Mozart, Esterhazy, Imperial, and Klimt. Then there's a divine specialty known as *Mohr im Hemd* (warm chocolate cake with fudge sauce) and of course the ubiquitous *Apfelstrudel* (apple strudel). If you can manage only one cake during your stay, make it the city's most famous indulgence—the irresistible chocolate *Sachertorte. See The Best Restaurants, p 109.*

❾ Take a tram-ride round the Ringstrasse. Catch Tram numbers 1 or 2 for a complete circuit of the epic boulevard surrounding the medieval city, trundling past a monumental assortment of palaces, parliament buildings, and grand hotels. *See The Ringstrasse tour, p 56.*

⑩ **Soak up the magical atmosphere of the Christmas markets.** Search for Christmas goodies, decorations, and beautifully carved cribs amid a winter wonderland of twinkling trees and snow-capped wooden huts. After buying your stocking-fillers, gather round the fireside for carols, *Glühwein*, and warm gingerbread. The main Christmas market takes place at Rathaus-Platz. *See p 60, bullet ❼.*

⑪ **Get lost in the maze of the Schönbrunn Palace.** Join the Viennese in one of their favorite pastimes—strolling in the Schönbrunn's magnificent formal gardens. This massive park is larger than the Principality of Monaco. Don't miss the zoo, tucked in one corner, with its adorable twin polar bears and panda; and Maria Theresa's grand apartments inside the palace. *See p 108, bullet ❺.*

⑫ **Party until the small hours at the nightspots under the arches of the U6 U-Bahn tracks and Gürtel highway.** As the trains roll overhead, enjoy the latest sounds from international DJs and top bands, including the very best in 'Viennese electronica'. End the night snacking on sausages from a streetside Wiener Würstelstand. *See The Gürtel Party tour, p 131.*

⑬ **Swim in the not-so "Blue Danube" and chill out on the beach.** Yes… there really is a beach in Vienna, and in summer it's packed with sunbathers, swimmers, and watersports fanatics. If you'd rather be on the water than in it, take a mini-cruise along the river. *See The Great Outdoors, p 93.*

⑭ **Pay homage to Vienna's musical *Wunderkind*.** Visit Mozart's house and hear his works at the celebrated Musikverein. Wherever you go in Vienna, you'll hear the strains of classical music emerging from open windows. Besides Mozart, Vienna was home to Haydn, Beethoven, Schubert, the Strausses, and many other musicians through the centuries. *See p 12 and 13, bullets ❹ & ❼.* ●

Johann Strauss—the most celebrated statue in town.

The Best of Vienna **in One Day**

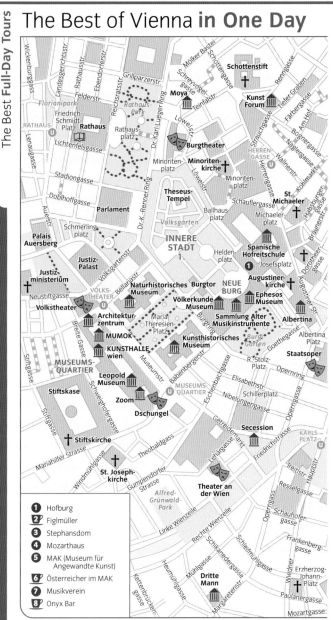

1 Hofburg
2 Figlmüller
3 Stephansdom
4 Mozarthaus
5 MAK (Museum für Angewandte Kunst)
6 Österreicher im MAK
7 Musikverein
8 Onyx Bar

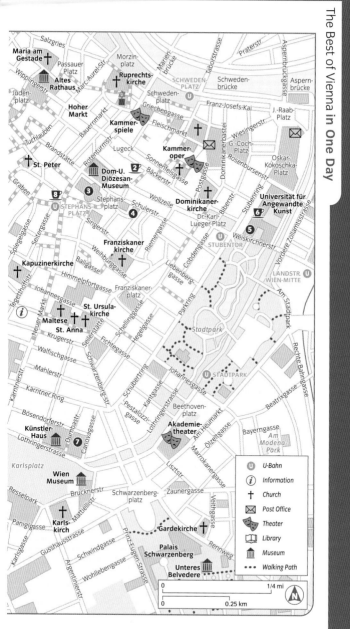

Legend:
- **U-Bahn**
- **Information**
- **Church**
- **Post Office**
- **Theater**
- **Library**
- **Museum**
- **Walking Path**

Scale:
- 0 — 1/4 mi
- 0 — 0.25 km

Where better to start exploring Vienna than at its historic heart? On this tour you can soak up the atmosphere of imperial Vienna; admire the Stephansdom (St Stephen's Cathedral and national emblem of Austria); tuck into the finest schnitzels in town; and take a reverential peep inside Mozart's only surviving Viennese home . . . all in a single day. START: **Hofburg (U-Bahn 3 Herrengasse).**

1 ★★★ **Hofburg.** Home to the powerful Habsburg dynasty which ruled Austria for six centuries, the grandiose Hofburg buildings are a remarkable long-term record of Viennese lifestyle and architecture. Don't be put off by the daunting tally of 18 wings, 19 courtyards, and 2,600 rooms. This rambling complex has been manageably packaged into neat clusters of attractions. The Sisi Museum vividly portrays the moving life of Vienna's beloved empress, Elisabeth of Bavaria (1837–98). The Imperial Apartments include the study, waiting room, and audience room of Sisi's husband, the Emperor Franz Joseph I (1848–1916). Sisi's exercise room contains some surprisingly modern gym apparatus. The Hofburg's first bathroom (which wasn't installed until 1876) featured the latest rage—a linoleum floor, while its tiny tiled closet was considered the last word in luxury at the time. Elsewhere within the vast Hofburg complex, make sure you don't miss the Schatzkammer (Treasury), a glittering hoard of Habsburg jewels amassed over more than a millennium, and the celebrated Spanische Reitschule (Spanish Riding School), where magnificent and beautiful Lipizzaner stallions cavort to Viennese waltz music. ⏱ *1–4 hr. Hofburg. www.hofburg-wien.at. U-Bahn 3 (Herrengasse). See p 28–31 and p 44, bullet* **5**.

2 ★★★ kids **Figlmüller.** Don't miss this cozy little restaurant, tucked down a narrow arcade. It's much visited by tourists and often very crowded, but it reputedly serves the best schnitzels in Vienna, bigger than a dinner-plate. These are traditionally accompanied by a mixed salad and wine from the owner's own vineyard in Grinzing (see p 103). Booking is essential. *Wollzeile 5.* ☎ *01 512 6177. $$.*

The Hofburg's central courtyard.

Sisi—A Tragic Empress

The eccentric, reclusive, and beautiful Empress 'Sisi' was born Elisabeth, Duchess of Bavaria, in 1837. At the tender age of 15, she agreed to marry her cousin, Franz Joseph of Austria, and took up residence in the Hofburg. Thrust unwillingly into the public eye, she hated imperial life and declined to fulfill the traditional roles of empress, wife, and mother. Her eldest child died aged two, and her fourth child committed suicide. She eventually became estranged from her husband, wrote increasingly melancholic poetry, and travelled incessantly. In 1885 she wrote: 'I am a seagull, of no land, I call no shore my home, I am bound to no place, I fly from wave to wave.' She was assassinated in Geneva in 1898 by an Italian anarchist, who later remarked: 'I wanted to kill a royal. It did not matter which one.'

❸ ★★ **Stephansdom.** The Viennese affectionately call their majestic cathedral the 'Steffl'. Dominating the city center, its skeletal spire towers 137m above the rooftops. Literally and figuratively, it represents a high point in Viennese Gothic architecture. The cathedral is now a national emblem. Its graceful pillars and lofty ribbed vaulting were described by architect Adolf Loos as 'the most spiritual church interior in the world'. Take the elevator (and your camera) up the north tower for exceptional views of the city center and the cathedral's eye-catching yellow, blue, and green rooftop, which consists of a quarter of a million brilliantly glazed tiles. The Stephansdom's 'Pummerin' (Boomer) bell is Austria's largest and heaviest. It is used just once annually—to ring in the New Year. Beethoven discovered the totality of his deafness when he realized he could no longer hear the bells. The square in front of the cathedral was once a marketplace. Medieval measuring marks are still visible in the masonry by the main west entrance. Two are ancient measures of length (the shorter 'Bohemian' and the longer 'Viennese' ell), while another indicates the correct size for a loaf of bread. 🕐 *1hr; go early on weekdays or during the evening to avoid the tour groups. Stephansplatz 3.* 📞 *01 515 52 3520. www.stephanskirche. at. Free admission. Mon–Sat 6am–10pm, Sun 7am–10pm. Elevator daily 8.30am–5.10pm (€4.50 adults,*

St. John Capistrano rallied the people to crusade in 1454 from this pulpit, to hold back the Muslim invasions of Christian Europe.

Stained glass window in the Museum of Applied Arts.

€1.50 kids). U-Bahn 1/3 (Stephansplatz).

4 ★★ **kids Mozarthaus.** There's no escaping Mozart's association with Vienna—from *Mozartkugeln* chocolates to ticket touts dressed in his typically flamboyant style. Of his fourteen addresses across the city, only the Mozarthaus remains—a most desirable residence even in Mozart's time. On arrival in Vienna in 1781, he wrote to his father 'This is a magnificent place here and the best place in the world for my profession'. He lived in this apartment from 1784 to 1787. They were his happiest and most productive years, during which time he composed countless chamber works and his opera *The Marriage of Figaro*. Here, Mozart's career reached its peak, but a taste for the highlife, especially gambling, ruined him. Just four years later, he died a pauper, buried in a mass grave in St Marx cemetery. It's well worth getting an audio guide here (there's a special one for kids too). Start at the top of the house and work your way down. Although lacking any of the composer's personal possessions, the house vividly portrays his life and times, through period furnishings

and musical memorabilia. ⏱ *1hr. Domgasse 5.* ☎ *01 512 1791. www. mozarthausvienna.at. €9 adults, €7 concessions, €7 students, €3 kids 3–12 (free under 3), €18 family (2 adults, 3 kids under 15); audio guides for adults and kids are included in the price. Daily 10am–7pm. U-Bahn 1/3 (Stephansplatz).*

5 ★★ **Museum für Angewandte Kunst (MAK).** The Applied Arts Museum is one of Vienna's most eclectic museums, showcasing eight centuries of Austrian decorative arts and design. Treasures range from Renaissance jewelry and Biedermeier furniture to the world's first fitted kitchen—the *Frankfurter Küche* (Frankfurt Kitchen). The rooms are arranged in chronological order from the Gothic era to the present day. Highlights include the Jugendstil (the German equivalent of the Art Nouveau movement) rooms, where the evolution of chair design is cleverly shown through a series of shadow screen silhouettes; and the exquisite Arts and Crafts exhibits from the Wiener Werkstätte

The view from Mozart's window down 'Bloody Alley'.

Musikverein façade.

(see p 35). Allow time to visit the superb museum shop, full of design objects, arty gifts and weird and wonderful gadgets and gizmos. ⏱ *1hr; the museum gets very crowded on Saturdays, when admission is free. Stubenring 5.* ☎ *01 711 36-0. www. mak.at. €7.90 adults, €5.50 concessions, €6.30 with Vienna Card, €11 family ticket (free under 6). Tues 10am–midnight, Wed–Sun 10am–6pm. U-Bahn 3 (Stubentor).*

6 ★★ **Österreicher im MAK.** This ultra-stylish, minimally furnished museum café with its elaborate coffered ceiling and big windows is the perfect venue for an early evening meal. Resident chef Helmut Österreicher's light, experimental cuisine offers a refreshing twist on the usual Viennese repertoire. If the weather's fine, ask for a table in the garden. *Stubenring 5.* ☎ *01 7144 0121. $$.*

7 ★★ **Musikverein.** If you can get to only one concert in Vienna, make sure it's at the Musikverein—the city's most prestigious classical

music venue. Each year, the sumptuously decorated Golden Hall hosts Vienna's celebrated New Year's Day concert, performed by its world-famous resident orchestra, the Vienna Philharmonic (see p 137). An awe-inspiring roll-call of former concert directors includes Johannes Brahms, Herbert von Karajan and, more recently, Leonard Bernstein, Claudio Abbado and Riccardo Muti. The building itself, designed by Theophil Hansen in Greek Renaissance style, with lavish use of terracotta capitals, balustrades, and gilded statuary, was opened in 1870 for the Viennese Society of Friends of Music. *Bösendorferstrasse 12.* ☎ *01 505 8190. www.musikverein.at. Tickets €4 (standing room)–€85. U-Bahn 1/2/4 (Karlsplatz).*

8 ★★ **Onyx Bar.** Enjoy a nightcap at this sleek rooftop bar in the curvaceous, hi-tech Haas Haus building (see p 63). The cocktail menu is almost as impressive as the photogenic views of the Stephansdom steeples. *Stephansplatz 12.* ☎ *01 5353 9690. $$.*

The Best of Vienna **in Two Days**

Wickenburggasse · Landesgerichtsstr. · Rathausstr. · Ebendorferstr. · Grillparzerstr. · Schreyvogel-gasse · Schottengasse · Mölker Bastei · Renngasse

Schottenstift †

Florianigasse · Friedrich-Schmidt-Platz · Reichsratsstr. · Felderstr. · Teinfaltstr. · Löwelstr.

Moya 🏛

Kunst Forum 🏛

Tiefer Graben · Färbergasse · Am Hof · Strauchgasse · Bognergasse · Naglergasse · Wallnerstr.

RATHAUS Ⓤ · Lenaugasse · Lichtenfelsgasse

Rathaus 📖

Rathaus-Park

Rathaus-platz

Dr.-Karl-Lueger-Ring

Burgtheater 🎭

HERREN-GASSE Ⓤ · Herrengasse

St. Michaeler †

Habsburgergasse · Kohlmarkt

Stadiongasse · Doblhoffgasse · Auerstr.

Parlament 🏛

Minoriten-platz · **Minoriten-kirche** † · Löwelstr. · Minoriten-platz · Schauflergasse · Michaeler-platz

Schmerling-platz · Dr.-K.-Renner-Ring · Reichsratsstr. · Bellariastr.

Theseus-Tempel

Ballhaus-platz

Volksgarten

HOFBURG

Palais Auersberg

Justiz-platz

INNERE STADT 1.

Helden-platz

Spanische Hofreitschule 🏛 · Josefsplatz

Dorotheer-gasse · Augustiner Str.

Justiz-ministerium † · Neustiftgasse

Justiz-Palast 🏛

VOLKS-THEATER Ⓤ · Volksgartenstr.

Naturhistorisches Museum 🏛 · Maria-Theresien-Platz

Burgtor

NEUE BURG 🏛

Augustiner-kirche † · **Ephesos Museum** 🏛

Volkstheater 🎭

Architektur-zentrum · **MUMOK** 🏛

Völkerkunde Museum 🏛

Burgring

Sammlung Alter Musikinstrumente 🏛

Albertina 🏛 · Albertina Platz

KUNSTHALLE wien 🏛 · **MUSEUMS-QUARTIER**

Museumstr.

7 **Burg-Garten**

Goethegasse · R.-Stolz-Platz

9 Opernring

Stiftskase

6 **Leopold Museum** 🏛

Babenbergerstr.

MUSEUMS-QUARTIER Ⓤ

Eschenbachgasse · Elisabethstr. · Nibelungengasse

Schillerplatz

Opernring · Operngasse

Stiftgasse · Schweighofergasse · Windmühlgasse

Zoom

Dschungel 🎭

Theobaldgasse

Getreidemarkt

Lehargasse

4 Friedrichstrasse

KARLS-PLATZ Ⓤ

† **Stiftskirche**

Mariahilfer Strasse

† **St. Joseph-kirche**

Alfred-Grünwald-Park

Theater an der Wien

5

Treitlstr. · Resselgasse · Hauptstr.

Linke Wienzeile · Rechte Wienzeile · Schikanedergasse · Schleifmühlgasse · Heumühlgasse · Mühlgasse · Margaretenstr.

Schauhofer-gasse · Frankenberg-gasse

Dritte Mann 🏛

Wiedner · Erzherzog-Johann-Platz

† **Paulanergasse**

Mozartgasse

- **1** Wien Museum
- **2** Karlskirche
- **3** Café Otto Wagner
- **4** Secession Building
- **5** Naschmarkt
- **6** MuseumsQuartier Wien
- **7** Burggarten (picnic)
- **8** KHM (Kunsthistorisches Museum) (minitour)
- **9** Staatsoper

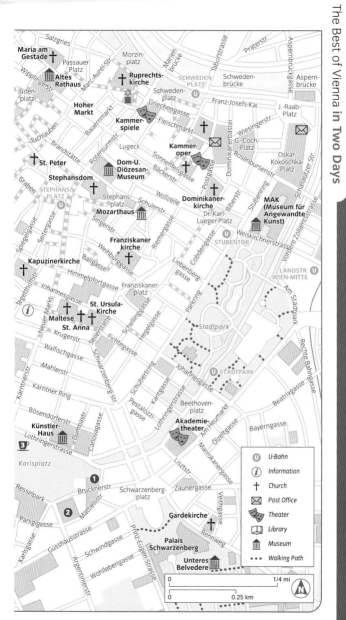

On your second day, you can start to get to the heart of the city. This tour unwraps more of Vienna's remarkable history and its dazzling art treasures, with a relaxing interlude to soak up the atmosphere and flavors of the Naschmarkt (Vienna's most colorful market). Some of the world's finest museums and art galleries await you after a snack or picnic lunch in the park. In the evening, a visit to the opera rounds off a perfect day. START: **U-Bahn 1/2/4 Karlsplatz.**

① ★★ Wien Museum. Don't let the ugly exterior of the Vienna Museum put you off. Inside, three floors trace the history of the city from the Neolithic Age to the mid-20th century, illustrated by some of its finest treasures. My favorite exhibits are the early maps and large-scale models of Vienna, showing vividly how the city has grown over the centuries. A clear overview of Vienna's eventful past makes exploring the city infinitely more rewarding. ⏱ *1hr. Karlsplatz.* ☎ *01 505 8747-0. www.wienmuseum.at. €6 adults, €4 concessions, €3 students, €13 family card (free on Sun). Tues–Sun 9am–6pm. U-Bahn 1/2/4 (Karlsplatz).*

② ★★ Karlskirche. This church is one of the most accomplished examples of the European baroque style, and deserves a close look both inside and out. Commissioned by Emperor Karl VI for the citizens of Vienna, this architectural masterpiece served to assert the Habsburg claim to European supremacy after the Siege of Vienna in 1683, when the Turks were finally driven from the empire. *See p 67, bullet* **⑤**.

③ Café Otto Wagner. Sit and watch the world go by in one of the former city railway stations (see p 33, bullet **②**), designed by pioneering Jugendstil architect Otto Wagner in 1899, now converted into a delightful café. *Karlsplatz.* ☎ *01 505 9904. $.*

④ ★★★ Secession Building. This unusual white block was created in 1898 by Otto Wagner's student, Joseph Maria Olbrich, as a 'Temple of Art'—a celebration of the 'Secessionist' artistic movement—reflecting the fluid, functional yet decorative style of a new generation of artists (led by Gustav Klimt) who rebelled against the meaningless excesses of Viennese ornamentation. An inscription above the door proclaims 'Der Zeit ihre Kunst, der Kunst ihre Freiheit' ('To the age, its own art; to art, its own freedom'). Garlands and floral patterns adorn

Karlskirche's imposing dome dominates the skyline.

Watch the world go by at the Café Otto Wagner.

the façade, while the entrance is decorated with a golden tree and the heads of the three Gorgons (representing architecture, sculpture, and painting). The crowning glory, however, is a dome of gilded laurel leaves—supposedly symbolizing the interdependence of art and nature—which has earned the Secession Building the affectionate nickname the 'Golden Cabbage'. The airy interior remains true to its original purpose, hosting exhibitions of contemporary art. In the basement, Klimt's Beethoven frieze is essential viewing (see p 33, bullet ❸).

🕐 *30min. Friedrichstrasse 12.* 📞 *01 587 5307. www.secession.at. €6 adults, €3.50 concessions (free under 10). Tues–Sun 10am–6pm, Thurs until 8pm; guided tours (in German) Sat 3pm, Sun 11am. U-Bahn 1/2/4 (Karlsplatz).*

❺ ★★★ **kids** **Naschmarkt.** The colorful Naschmarkt is Vienna's largest and liveliest market—a must for all food lovers and perfect place to look for picnic provisions. Mouth-watering displays of seasonal produce—fruit, vegetables, flowers, fish, cheese, and wine—give visitors an extraordinary culinary tour around the world. It stands in the valley of the River Wien, a site once occupied by medieval vineyards and an 18th-century milk market. Traditional wooden stalls lend it an old-fashioned air. It also has a dazzling choice of eateries to suit all tastes and budgets, ranging from the snack bars which kick-start market traders with early-morning caffeine shots to seafood brasseries that seduce city sophisticates with platters of oysters. The Karlsplatz end tends to have the smartest (and most expensive) Viennese-run stalls, along with luxury delicatessens and elegant pavement cafés. This gives way to a less formal multi-ethnic

Tempting displays at the Naschmarkt draw crowds of shoppers daily.

section, selling exotic produce and spices from all over the world. Further west (near Kettenbrücken-gasse), a popular farmers' market takes place on Fridays and Saturdays (Mar–Oct), and a Saturday morning fleamarket hawks a jumble of antiques, clothing, and bric-a-brac to bargain hunters. ⏱ *1hr. Naschmarkt. Stalls: Mon–Fri 8am–6pm, Sat 6am–1pm; snack bars: times vary, some open until 10pm or 11pm, closed Sun. U-Bahn 1/2/4 (Karlsplatz), U-Bahn 4 (Kettenbrückengasse).*

6 ★★★ **kids** **Museums-Quartier Wien.** Built as 'an urban cultural oasis' and housed within former riding stables dating from baroque times, this huge museum complex is one of the great success stories of contemporary Vienna. Several art galleries surround a vast central courtyard. The Leopold Museum contains Austrian art from the 19th and 20th centuries; MUMOK is the nation's largest modern-art museum; and the Kunsthalle stages temporary art exhibitions. Add to this an architecture center, a kids' museum, and a cluster of shops, open-air restaurants, cafés and bars, and you have one of the most popular cultural venues in town for locals and visitors alike (see p 74). ⏱ *1–6hr. Museumsplatz 1.* ☎ *01 523 81-1730. www.mqw.at. U-Bahn 2 (Museumsquartier).*

7 ★ **kids** **Picnic lunch in Burggarten.** Join Mozart, Goethe, and other sculpted luminaries in this shady park (see p 58, bullet **2**) and tuck in to your Naschmarkt picnic; or snatch a sausage with crusty bread and a dollop of mustard from the Wienerwürstlstand by the main entrance to the park. *Burgring, opposite Eschenbachgasse. No phone. $.*

8 ★★★ **Kunsthistorisches Museum (KHM).** Vienna's superlative Museum of Fine Arts occupies a monumental Renaissance-style building on the Ringstrasse. It contains the Imperial collection assembled over centuries by the Habsburgs, who were keen patrons and avid collectors of art. It's a staggering haul of treasures from all around the world, displayed in room after room on three floors. There's far too much to see properly in a single visit, be sure to see the Old Master paintings in the Gemäldegalerie (Picture Gallery) on the first floor.

9 ★★★ **Staatsoper.** The State Opera holds a special place in the hearts of the Viennese, and is recognized by music-lovers everywhere as one of the world's most illustrious opera-houses. You can visit the interior, with its grand staircase and plush red-and-gold auditorium, on a guided

Egyptian friezes adorn the walls of the KHM.

Kunsthistorisches Museum Vienna

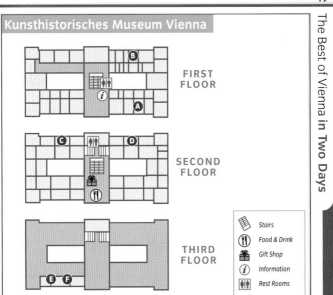

FIRST FLOOR

SECOND FLOOR

THIRD FLOOR

📖	Stairs
🍴	Food & Drink
🎁	Gift Shop
ⓘ	Information
🚻	Rest Rooms

Start on the ground floor in the **8A** **Ancient Egyptian collection**, to see the mummies (Room I), Ka-Ni-Nisut's ancient tomb (Room II), the statue of King Thutmosis III and a charming blue ceramic hippopotamus (both Room IX). In **8B** **Greek and Roman Antiquities**, look out for the impressive 2nd-century mosaic of *Theseus and the Minotaur* (Room XII), exquisite Roman cameos (Room XVI), and rare textiles (Room XVIII). The first-floor picture gallery represents all the major schools of European art and many of the world's greatest artists too. **8C** **German, Flemish, and Dutch paintings** include Brueghel the Elder's *The Seasons* cycle (Room X), Dürer's *Madonna with the Pear* (Room 16),

Rembrandt's *Large Self-Portrait* (Room 21), and Vermeer's *The Art of Painting* (Room 22). **8D** **Italian and Spanish paintings** feature Archimboldo's extraordinary *Seasons* and *Elements* paintings (Room 7), and Velazquez's portrait of the eight-year-old *Infanta Margarita Teresa in Blue Dress* (Room 10), who married Leopold I just seven years later. The paintings of early 18th-century imperial palaces and Viennese views by Canaletto's nephew Bellotto commissioned for the Empress Maria Theresa (Room VII) are especially fascinating. The second floor contains one of the world's most extensive **8E** **coin collections** and over 1,000 **8F** **miniature portraits** collected by Emperor Ferdinand II.

tour. Even if you wouldn't normally consider seeing an opera, you may well be lured by the glitz and glamour of the Staatsoper. If you do, try to make Mozart your first performance.

🕐 *40min tour (start times vary but are usually advertised on a board at the entrance daily). Opernring 2.* 📞 *01 514-44 7810 (box office). www. staatsoper.at. Tram 1/2/D/J (Oper).*

The Best of Vienna **in Three Days**

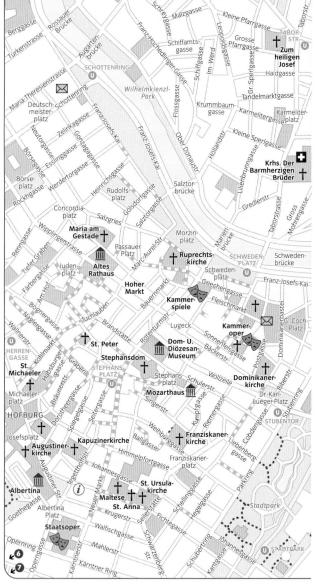

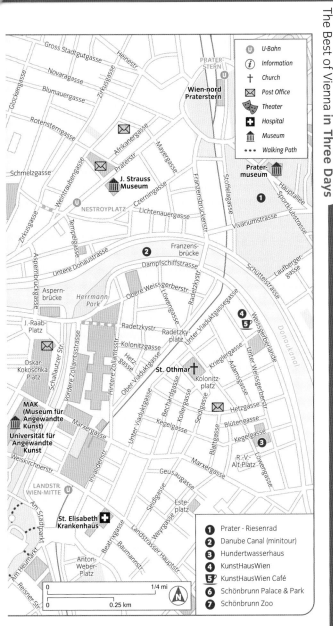

Legend:

- U U-Bahn
- (i) Information
- † Church
- ✉ Post Office
- 🎭 Theater
- ✚ Hospital
- 🏛 Museum
- ••• Walking Path

1. Prater - Riesenrad
2. Danube Canal (minitour)
3. Hundertwasserhaus
4. KunstHausWien
5. KunstHausWien Café
6. Schönbrunn Palace & Park
7. Schönbrunn Zoo

After two days of art, architecture, history, and culture, today's trip takes in some of the city's best-loved attractions, including the famous Prater Riesenrad (ferris wheel), some eccentric modern architecture, the city zoo, and Schönbrunn, the most-visited palace in Austria. It requires an early start and a bit of stamina, but you will be well rewarded for your efforts. Don't forget your camera!
START: **U-Bahn 1 (Praterstern).**

1 ★★★ kids **Prater (Riesenrad).** See p 98, bullet **4**.

2 ★★ kids **Danube Canal cruise.** The Danube, Vienna's lifeblood since Roman times, was partly canalized at the end of the 19th century to reduce flooding in the built-up areas of the city. A mini-cruise provides an entirely new perspective of the city. The DDSG (Blue Danube Shipping Company) offers two short trips or a round tour. My favorite route is Strecke A (Stretch A), which takes just under two hours (starting from Schwedenplatz), and passes some of Vienna's lesser known but nonetheless intriguing sights.

3 ★★ kids **Hundertwasserhaus.** You can't fail to spot the quirky Hundertwasserhaus! With its

See the sights by boat.

The Prater amusement park—fun for all the family.

vividly-colored patchwork façade, gleaming gold onion-domes, distinct lack of straight lines (even inside) and tree-clad roof, this building stands out among the dull Austro-Hungarian empire architecture that surrounds it. Designed by Austrian artist, Friedensreich Hundertwasser in 1986 as a public housing complex, it provoked fierce debate among the Viennese who described it as 'an unbearable display of new-money pomposity.' Now it is a much loved part of the Viennese cityscape. *Löwengasse (on the corner of Kegelgasse). www.hundertwasserhaus.at. Tram N (Hetzgasse).*

4 ★★★ kids **KunstHausWien.** Just round the corner from the Hundertwasserhaus is one of my favorite

Danube Canal

The first eye-catching sight on this tour is the cupola of the **2A** ★ **Sternwarte Urania.** Built in 1910, this Austria's oldest astronomical observatory and also contains a cinema, puppet theater and a café with superb canal vistas. Further east, look out for glimpses of the **2B** ★★★ **KunstHausWien** (See p 22, bullet **4**), designed by Vienna's radical architect, Hundertwasser. Beyond lies a curious structure known as the **2C** ★ **Gasometer**. These four rotund brick towers were used to store the city's gas supply from 1899 to 1969. In the 1990s, they were converted into 615 apartments, a vast shopping center, and leisure complex. As you pass through the massive Freudenau lock

on to the New Danube, you'll see the gravel beaches of the Donauinsel (Danube Island) to your right and the **2D** **Prater** park (see p 96) on your left. Look out for three Prater landmarks: the Buddhist pagoda; the Ernst Happel Stadium (venue of the Euro 2008 football tournament); and the Riesenrad (see p 98, bullet **4**). The tour ends at the Reichsbrücke, a bridge near Mexikoplatz. The most prominent building on this square is the multi-turreted **2E** **Franz-von-Assisi-Kirche**, built in 1898 by Emperor Franz Joseph I to commemorate his golden anniversary. *DDSG Information Desk, Handelskai 265. ☎ 01 58880. www.ddsg-blue-danube.at. U-Bahn 1 (Vorgartenstrasse).*

museums—the KunstHausWien. This is not your usual museum experience but rather an adventure of creative architecture, and the chance to

experience the extraordinary range of Hundertwasser's creative genius, which encompassed art, graphics, models, tapestry, kites, sculpture,

KunstHausWien, designed by the undeniably eccentric Friedensreich Hundertwasser.

shiny, irregularly shaped pillars; a roof garden and no straight lines (even the floor is uneven). When it was created in 1989, critics described it as 'tasteless', resembling 'a half-melted slab of liquorice'. Come and see what you think.

🕐 *1hr. Morning is the quietest time to visit; avoid weekends if possible. Untere Weissgerberstrasse 13. ☎ 01 712 0495. www.kunsthauswien.com. €9 adults, €7 concessions, €3 kids. €20 family. Daily 10am–7pm. Tram N/O (Radestzkyplatz).*

5 ★★★ **kids** **KunstHausWien Café.** As you might expect from Hundertwasser, this café is quirky and informal, with a delightful shaded patio area. Its simple menu includes a good choice of vegetarian dishes. *Untere Weissgerberstrasse 13. ☎ 01 712 0495. $–$$.*

even postage stamps. His brightly colored paintings are as distinctive as his architectural constructions. The building (a converted furniture factory) features all the artist's characteristic trademarks—vivid colors contrasting with black and gold;

6 ★★★ **kids** **Schönbrunn Palace & Park.** See p 104.

7 ★★ **kids** **Schönbrunn Zoo.** See p 108, bullet **7**. ●

Hundertwasser

When the flamboyant Friedensreich Hundertwasser (1928–2000) left the Vienna Academy of Fine Arts in 1948 after just three months of study, it seemed unlikely that he would become one of Austria's most celebrated (albeit controversial) artist-designers. He felt that design was stagnant ('our real illiteracy is our inability to create') and in an effort similar to the Secessionist movement 100 years previously, he strove to find harmony between nature and the creativity of man. His style frequently reflected two of his beliefs in particular: that 'the straight line is alien to mankind' and 'our whole life proceeds in spirals'. He made his mark on Vienna with the Hundertwasserhaus, the KunstHausWien, and one of Vienna's oddest tourist attractions—the Fernwärme—Europe's brightest municipal rubbish incinerator out at Spittelau (*U-Bahn 6 Spittelau*).

Imperial Vienna

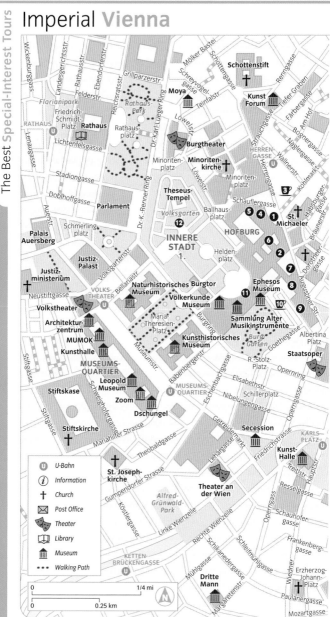

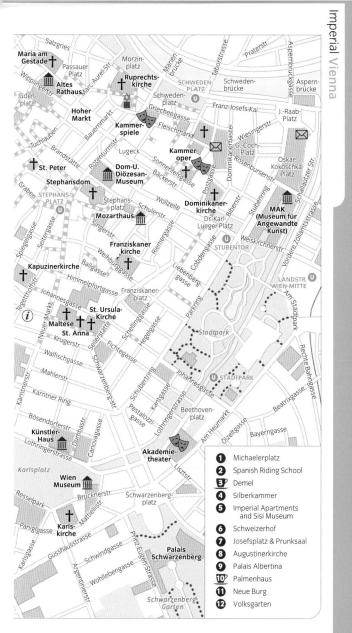

1 Michaelerplatz
2 Spanish Riding School
3 Demel
4 Silberkammer
5 Imperial Apartments and Sisi Museum
6 Schweizerhof
7 Josefsplatz & Prunksaal
8 Augustinerkirche
9 Palais Albertina
10 Palmenhaus
11 Neue Burg
12 Volksgarten

The Hofburg, residence of the mighty Habsburg dynasty for over 600 years, should be on every visitor's itinerary. Originally a medieval castle, it was extended by each successive emperor to demonstrate the power and riches of the Habsburgs, until it effectively became a 'city within a city'. The resulting labyrinthine complex, and the astounding treasures within it, established Vienna's reputation worldwide as a place of unrivalled elegance, wealth, and splendor.

1 ★ **Michaelerplatz.** Layer upon layer of history has been unearthed in Michaelerplatz, the monumental square adjacent to the Hofburg. Roman remains and medieval foundations were recently excavated at the centre of the square. Then there's the grandly colonnaded Michaelertrakt (St. Michael's Wing) and Michaelertor (St. Michael's Gate) entrance to the Hofburg—both added by Emperor Franz Joseph in 1893. The fountains on the outer limits of the main gateway (see below) symbolize Habsburg power both on land and at sea. The gigantic copper-clad cupola above the Michaelertor looks especially striking (and photogenic) from

Mastery of the Seas sculpture in Michaelerplatz.

Kohlmarkt. The Michaelerkirche opposite was once the parish church of the Imperial Court (*see p 55, bullet* **7**). Also in the square, Loos Haus (designed by Adolf Loos) broke architectural boundaries in 1912 with its functional design and unadorned green marble façade (*see p 34, bullet* **7**).

2 ★★★ **kids Spanish Riding School.** *See p 44, bullet* **5**.

3 **Demel.** This charming café and cake shop named after the imperial confectioner was founded in 1786. For centuries it has drawn wealthy Viennese shoppers to its old-fashioned mirrored and gilded interior for exquisite coffee, cakes, and confectionery, including Empress Sisi's favorite, sugared violets. *Kohlmarkt 14.* ☎ *01 5351717–0. $$.*

4 ★★ **Silberkammer.** The Imperial Silver Collection is a dazzling array of priceless tableware in glass, silver, and porcelain. Some of these precious pieces are still used today for state banquets. The Grand Vermeil dinner service (Room 7), containing 4,500 pieces, is one of the world's largest silver-gilt services. Porcelain highlights include the flower plates of keen botanist, Emperor Franz II (Room D); the Hunting Lodge porcelain given by Sisi to Franz Joseph in 1870 (Room

Traditional costumes on display in Franz Josef's waiting room.

6); floral baroque Meissen, Minton, and Sèvres porcelain services (Rooms H and J); and 60 pictorial plates from the Viennese Manufactory (Room 23), decorated with local scenes, including Schönbrunn, Belvedere, and Prater. ⏱ *45 min. Hofburg.* ☎ *01 533 7570. www. hofburg-wien.at. €9.90 adults, €4.90 kids (6–18), €8.90 concessions. Audio guides available free of charge. Ticket price includes the Sisi Museum and Imperial Apartments. Daily 9am–5pm (5.30pm July–Aug). Arrive before opening time to beat the crowds in high season. U-Bahn 3 (Herrengasse).*

5 ★★★ **kids** **Imperial Apartments and Sisi Museum.** The Imperial Palace accommodated the Habsburg royals for over six centuries (1282-1918), during which time the Hofburg complex developed into one of the great powerhouses of Europe. The first six rooms form the Sisi Museum, where a host of artifacts (poems, recipes, dresses, toiletries, portraits, jewelry,

and so forth) offer a fascinating insight into the tragic empress's private life. Some items reveal her passions for travel, poetry and sport, as well as her obsession with beauty and diet. Among her favorite beauty treatments were a leather facemask lined in raw veal and worn overnight, and a shampoo recipe for egg yolk and cognac to wash her floor-length hair—a process that took all day. From her early 30s onwards she refused to allow her portrait to be painted, so that she would always be remembered as a great beauty. ⏱ *1hr; visit early to avoid the crowds. Hofburg.* ☎ *01 533 7570. www.hofburg-wien.at. €9.90 adults, €4.90 kids (6–18), €8.90 concessions. Audio guides available free of charge. Ticket price includes the Sisi Museum & Imperial Apartments. Daily 9am–5pm (5.30pm July–Aug); kids' tours: 10.30am, 2.30pm Sat, Sun and public holidays. U-Bahn 3 (Herrengasse).*

6 ★★★ **kids** **Schweizerhof (Swiss Court).** The oldest part of

The grandiose Imperial Library.

the Hofburg, the Swiss Court, was originally a 13th-century fortress complete with a moat and draw-bridge, built by King Ottokar of Bohemia to defend himself against Rudolf von Habsburg. He failed, and the Habsburgs moved in. The name recalls the Swiss Guards who were once posted here. Enter through the striking red, black, and gold **Schweizertor** (Swiss Gate), one of Vienna's finest Renaissance constructions, into the ancient

courtyard. The Gothic **Burgkapelle** (Castle Chapel), up the steps to your right, was restored in baroque style in the 17th and 18th centuries. Mass is famously performed here every Sunday (except July–Sept) by the **Wiener Sängerknaben** (Vienna Boys' Choir—see p 137). The sparkling **Schatzkammer** (Treasury), whose entrance is beneath the chapel, is one of the world's most impressive national collections, containing a breath-taking hoard of jewels, crowns, and sacred relics spanning 1,000 years of both the Habsburg and the Holy Roman empires. 🕐 *Schatzkammer: ¾ hr. Hofburg.* ☎ *01 525 24-0. www.khm. at, www.hofburgkapelle.at.* €10 *adults,* €7.50 *concessions,* €3.50 *kids,* €20 *family card (2 adults plus up to 3 kids),* €3 *audio guide. Wed–Mon 10am–6pm. (chapel: €1.50. Open Mon–Thurs 11am–3pm, Fri 11am–1pm) U-Bahn 3 (Herrengasse).*

⑦ ★ Josefsplatz. An equestrian statue of Emperor Joseph II marks the center of this sun-baked square, once used as a training ground for the Spanish Riding School. It is flanked by two fine palaces, the Renaissance **Stallburg** (stables) and

The mighty equestrian statue of Franz Josef dominates the entrance to the Albertina.

Dine in the emperors' greenhouse—the Palmenhaus!

the **Prunksaal** (State Hall). This magnificent building is a gem of baroque architecture, decked with marble statuary, nutwood bookcases, and lavish frescoes. Once the Imperial Library, it remains the largest room of its kind in Europe, and contains a major part of the National Library's extensive collection of manuscripts, maps, books, and music scores. ⏱ *20min. Prunksaal, Josefsplatz 1. www.onb.ac.at. €5 adults, €3 concessions. Tues–Sun 10am–6pm (until 9pm Thurs). Guided tour: Thurs 6pm (€2). U-Bahn 3 (Herrengasse).*

8 ★ **Augustinerkirche.** *See Best Churches p 55, bullet* **5**.

9 ★★ **Palais Albertina.** One of the world's finest collections of graphic art is housed in the Albertina Palace at the southern end of the Hofburg. Named after Duke Albert of Saxony-Teschen, it contains his extensive collection of a million etchings, engravings and lithographs, over 65,000 watercolors

and drawings, and around 70,000 photographs. Virtually every major artist from the 15th century to the present day is represented. Highlights include works by Dürer, Michelangelo, Rembrandt, and Rubens. There are no permanent exhibitions; the artworks are rotated in temporary displays due to their sensitivity to light. Since its reopening in 2003, following extensive renovation, the magnificent neoclassical Habsburg State Rooms of the Palais Albertina are now open to the public for the first time in 200 years. ⏱ *1hr; quietest over lunch-hour. Albertinaplatz 1.* ☎ *01 534 83-0. www.albertina.at. €9.50 adults, €8 concessions, €7 students, €3.50 kids (free under 6). Daily 10am–6pm (until 9pm Wed). U-Bahn 1/2/4 (Karlsplatz).*

10 ★★ **Palmenhaus.** You'll love the beautiful Jugendstil Palmenhaus (Glass House) brasserie in the former Imperial Garden. It is a stylish setting for lunch, serving delicious Viennese and Mediterranean dishes and fine wines. *Burggarten.* ☎ *01 533 1033. $$–$$$. Tram 1/2/D/J (Burgring).*

11 ★ **Neue Burg.** *See p 60, bullet* **5**.

12 ★ **Volksgarten.** This beautiful garden between Heldenplatz (see p 47, bullet **5**) and the Burgtheater (see p 60, bullet **8**) is surely Vienna's most romantic, famed for its beautiful roses (each carefully labeled) and its Theseus temple, built for Sisi in 1822 as a gift from her husband, Franz Joseph. ⏱ *30 min. Tram 1/2/D/J (Dr-Karl-Renner-Ring).*

Jugendstil Vienna

Legend:
- U-Bahn
- (i) Information
- + Church
- ⊠ Post Office
- Theater
- Museum
- ··· Walking Path

1. Upper Belvedere
2. Otto Wagner Pavilions
3. Secession
4. Naschmarkt
5. Wagner Apartments
6. Leopold Museum
7. Loos Haus
8. MAK (Museum für Angewandte Kunst)
9. Postsparkasse
10. American Bar

Vienna is the birthplace of Jugendstil—Austria's answer to Art Nouveau—and its spin-off movement, the **Secession**. This tour takes you on a 'greatest-hits' trip around their ground-breaking, Modernist art and architecture, including the *pièce de résistance*, the Secession Building—a daring structure with a cupola of golden laurel leaves, known locally as the 'Golden Cabbage'.

① ★★★ Upper Belvedere.

The best collection of Austrian Modernism can be found in the Belvedere (www.belvedere.at), a glorious baroque palace, where pride of place goes to the celebrated work known as *The Kiss* by Gustav Klimt (founder of the Secession movement), alongside paintings by French Impressionists and Austrian contemporaries Schiele and Kokoschka. *See p 68, bullet ⑧.*

② ★★ Otto Wagner Pavilions.

These two symmetrical Jugendstil railway stations were built as part of Otto Wagner's scheme for Vienna's horse-drawn rail network. Made of green-painted steel with white marble slabs, they have striking decorative golden flower motifs. Both stations fell into disuse when the modern U-Bahn was built. They

The sunflower motif on Wagner's pavilions is a recurring Jugendstil theme.

The striking Secession building.

were dismantled in the 1960s but re-erected in 1977, following extensive protests. One is now a café (see p 16, bullet ③); the other contains a small museum devoted to Wagner. ⏱ *20min. Karlsplatz.* ☎ *01 505 874 785 177. www.wienmuseum.at. €2 adults, €1 concessions, free on Sun. Apr–Oct, Tues–Sun 9am–6pm. U-Bahn 1/2/4 (Karlsplatz).*

③ ★★★ Secession.

This gallery is the finest example of Jugendstil architecture in Vienna, reflecting the Secessionist ideals of purity and functionalism. Be sure to visit the fascinating interior, if only to see Gustav Klimt's remarkable 34m-long Beethoven frieze in the basement. Based on the composer's 9th Symphony (and, in particular, his musical setting of German poet Schiller's

Wagner's ornate Majolikahaus.

Ode to Joy), it is one of the masterpieces of Viennese Art Nouveau. *See p 16, bullet* ④.

④ ★★★ **kids** **Naschmarkt.** You'll find some of the best snack bars in the city at Vienna's top market, serving everything from Wienerwurst to sushi and satay. My favorites include the **Naschmarkt Deli** for brunch (Stand 421-436, ☎ 01 585 0823, $); **Umar Fisch** (Stand 76, ☎ 01 587 0456, $$) for shellfish; and the **Indian Pavillion** (stand 74-75, ☎ 01 587 8561, $–$$) for a taste of the exotic. *See The Best Dining, p 109.*

⑤ ★ **Wagner Apartments.** Few façades in Vienna are as beautiful as the Jugendstil MajolikaHaus. Designed by pioneering architect Otto Wagner in 1899, it is named after the majolica tiles he used to create the colorful, flowing, floral patterns covering the exterior. Together with its neighbor (on the corner of Köstlergasse), whose curvaceous façade is further embellished with gold embossing by Secessionist artist Koloman Moser,

they represent Wagner's ultimate fusion of Art Nouveau decoration with modern materials. ⏱ *5min. Linke Wienzeile 40 and 38.* ☎ *No phone. Closed to the public. U-Bahn 4 (Kettenbrückengasse).*

⑥ ★★★ **Leopold Museum.** The main draw of this gallery of 19th- and 20th-century Austrian art is the world's largest collection of works by the provocative artist, Egon Schiele. It also contains some significant Klimt canvases. While you're here, check out the exquisite Arts and Crafts furniture designs of the Wiener Werkstatte. *See p 76, bullet* ②.

⑦ ★ **Loos Haus.** Loos Haus, designed by Adolf Loos in 1921, caused an outcry when it was first built. Its austere design, geometric lines, and lack of ornamentation offended public taste during a period when florid façades were still *de rigueur*. The ornament-loving Emperor Franz Joseph found the house so hideous that he kept the curtains of rooms overlooking Michaelerplatz drawn shut and refused to use the Hofburg's Michaelertor exit ever again. Nicknamed 'the house without eyebrows', it is now

Fiaker passing Loos Haus—the 'house without eyebrows'.

The Wiener Werkstätte

The Wiener Werkstätte (Viennese Workshop), founded in 1903 by Josef Hoffmann and Koloman Moser as a direct offshoot of the Secession movement, was inspired by the Arts and Crafts movement, popular in Britain at the time. The aim was to bring Jugendstil design into homes throughout Vienna. By turning functional, everyday objects such as cutlery, crockery, furniture, and curtains into unique items of great beauty and quality, they sought to transform daily life into a 'Gesamtkunstwerk' (total work of art). By 1905, the Wiener Werkstätte had over 100 craftsmen, including Klimt, Loos, and Kokoschka, but it was forced to close in 1932, unable to compete financially with the cheap, mass-produced items made by rival companies. Nowadays, the best collections of Wiener Werkstätte artifacts can be seen in the Leopold Museum and MAK (see p 12, bullet ❺). Some upmarket design shops still sell products along similar lines, notably Augarten, Lobmeyr, Woka, and Thonet (see The Best Shopping, p 79).

considered a masterpiece of modern design. The interior (currently a bank) reflects the exterior's simple, stylish elegance. ⏱ *10min. Herrengasse 2–4.* ☎ *No phone. www.designzone looshaus.at. Bank opening hours (to glimpse inside): Mon–Wed, Fri 9am–3pm, Thurs 9am–5.30pm. U-Bahn 3 (Herrengasse).*

❽ ★★ **Museum für Angewandte Kunst (MAK).** The Jugendstil and Wiener Werkstätte rooms are a must-see here. *See p 12, bullet ❺.*

❾ ★ **Postsparkasse.** This marvelous example of Secession architecture was designed by Otto Wagner in 1904–6. He won a competition to create a novel structure capable of reflecting the Post Office Savings Bank's innovative procedures, and came up with this extraordinary gray marble façade, held together by 17,000 metal studs and topped by stylized Jugendstil

angels. The lofty, light-infused interior (and tiny Wagner museum) can be viewed during bank opening times. ⏱ *10min (30min including museum). Georg-Coch-Platz 2.* ☎ *01 534 533 3088. www.ottowagner.at. Museum: €5 adults, €3.50 concessions (free under 6). Mon, Thurs 8.30am–8.30pm, Tues–Wed, Fri 8.30am–3pm, Sat 10am–5pm. U-Bahn 1/4 (Schwedenplatz).*

❿ ★★ **American Bar.** Designed by Adolf Loos in 1908, this cocktail bar is an absolute gem, characterized by clever use of mirrors (to create an illusion of space), beautiful Art Nouveau glass cabinets, onyx, marble, and—a Loos' hallmark— mahogany paneling. Come for early evening drinks, before the crowds arrive. *Kärntner Durchgang 10.* ☎ *01 512 3283. www.loosbar.at. U-Bahn 1/3 (Stephansplatz).*

City of Music

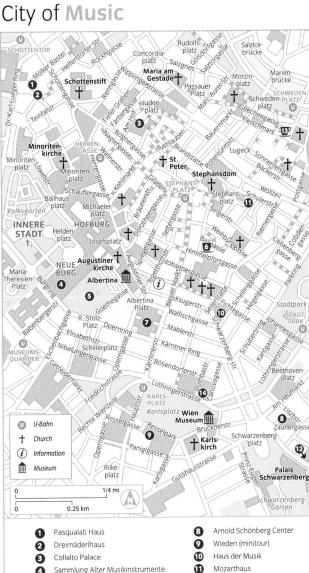

U	U-Bahn
†	Church
(i)	Information
🏛	Museum

```
0           1/4 mi
0      0.25 km
```

❶	Pasqualati Haus
❷	Dreimäderlhaus
❸	Collalto Palace
❹	Sammlung Alter Musikinstrumente
❺	Burggarten
❻	Café Frauenhuber
❼	Staatsoper
❽	Arnold Schönberg Center
❾	Wieden (minitour)
❿	Haus der Musik
⓫	Mozarthaus
⓬	Central Cemetery
⓭	Griechenbeisl
⓮	Musikverein

This lengthy but fascinating tour pieces together the extraordinary legacy of one of the world's leading musical cities from Mozart the musical whiz-kid to the kings of the Viennese waltz. It also includes some lesser known sights and historic buildings closed to the public, which you can easily skip if you are short of time or energy.

Pasqualati House—one of Beethoven's numerous residences.

1 ★★ **Pasqualati Haus.** The German-born composer Ludwig van Beethoven moved to Vienna at the age of 22 to take lessons with Haydn and Mozart. During his 35 years in the city, he moved house a staggering 68 times. The Pasqualati house on the old city ramparts (named after its long-time owner Josef von Pasqualati) is the most interesting of three Beethoven houses currently open to the public. The composer lived in this house from 1804 to 1818, and wrote many of his best-loved works here, including the opera *Fidelio*, Symphonies 4, 5, 7, and 8, and his 4th piano concerto. His rooms (on the 4th floor) contain just a handful of mementoes, portraits, scores, and personal belongings, but they are wonderfully evocative. In the back room, enjoy listening to excerpts of his 'greatest hits' while gazing over the city rooftops. When Beethoven lived here, he would have had sweeping views of the Vienna Woods. ⏱ *45min. Mölker Bastei 8.* ☎ *01 535 8905. www.wienmuseum. at. €6 adults, €4 concessions, €3 kids, €13 family ticket; free on Sun. Tues–Sun 10am–1pm, 2pm–6pm. U-Bahn 2 (Schottentor).*

2 ★ **Dreimäderlhaus.** *See p 72, bullet* **5**.

3 ★ **Collalto Palace.** Even though you can't go inside, all Mozart fans make their pilgrimage to see the simple plaque on the wall of the unremarkable baroque building situated in Vienna's largest enclosed square. It commemorates the site where Mozart made his first public appearance, aged just six, in 1762. The boy-wonder had recently arrived by boat from his native Salzburg and wowed the audience with his mastery of the clavichord and violin. *Am Hof 13. U-Bahn 3 (Herrengasse).*

4 ★ **Sammlung Alter Musikinstrumente.** It seems fitting that such a musically-rich city should have an impressive musical instrument collection, and you won't be disappointed by this collection of Ancient Musical Instruments. Started by Archduke Ferdinand of Tyrol, this now contains the finest ensemble of Renaissance instruments in the world, including an extraordinary 16th-century claviorgan, which can

An Italian 19th century mandolin in the Sammlung Alter Musikinstrumente.

reproduce special effects like bird-song; some early serpents (snake-shaped horns); violins with elaborately carved scrolls; and pianos once owned by Haydn, Beethoven, and Schubert. ⏱ 45min. Neue Burg, Heldenplatz. ☎ 01 525 24–4602. www.khm.at. €8 adults, €6 concessions, €3 kids, €16 family; price includes admission to the Ephesus Museum and Arms and Armor Collection; €3 audio guide. Wed–Mon 10am–6pm. Tram 1/2/D/J (Ringstrasse).

5 ★★ **kids**
Burggarten. This informal park in the city center (see p 58, bullet **2**) contains a magnificent marble statue of Mozart by Viktor Tilgner (1896), and scenes in bas-reliefs from his opera Don Giovanni. Burgring (just inside the main gates, opposite Eschenbach-gasse). Tram 1/2/D/J (Ringstrasse).

Mozart graces the Burggarten.

6 ★ **Café Frauenhuber.** Fortify yourself with coffee and cake in Vienna's oldest café. Mozart once lived in this building, and Beethoven used to perform piano sonatas here. Himmelpfortgasse 6. ☎ 01 512 8383. $–$$.

7 ★★★ **Staatsoper.** Vienna's reputation as a 'City of Music' focuses largely on its prestigious State Opera, which has for centuries staged premieres of many leading works. It continues to enjoy a dazzling reputation, with 300 performances annually taken from its vast repertoire of ballets and opera 'greats' (including Mozart's The Magic Flute, Wagner's Ring Cycle, and Beethoven's Fidelio). It is also the venue for the annual Opera Ball, the most glittering event in the Austrian social calendar, held on the last Thursday of Vienna's Fasching (Carnival) season celebrations. Stage and stalls are transformed into a gigantic flower-filled ballroom. I thoroughly recommend a guided tour of the interior, for a closer look at its grand staircase and plush red-and-gold auditorium. Tour times vary depending on rehearsal schedules, but they are usually advertised on a daily billboard by the entrance. ⏱ 40min tour. Opernring 2. ☎ 01 514 44–7810 (box office). www.staatsoper. at. Tram 1/2/D/J (Oper).

8 ★★ **Arnold Schönberg Center.** Somewhat off the tourist track, this small archive center is essential viewing for any aficionado of 20th-century classical music (see Jewish

The Viennese Waltz

The plodding, triple-time German folk dance known as the Ländler was transformed by the Viennese into a merry, whirling dance during the 1820s. It first became popular in Viennese dance-halls thanks to the composer and leader of a small ensemble, Joseph Lanner. Johann Strauss I (also known as 'the Elder') was one of his viola players and, in 1825, he broke away to form his own waltz orchestra. The two band-leaders conducted a lengthy 'waltz war', performing in the cafés of the Prater, but the rivalry ended amicably when Strauss played waltz tunes (at slow speed) at Lanner's funeral in 1843. After his death, the Strauss family dominated the Viennese waltz scene for over half a century—thanks largely to Johann Strauss II, the second-generation 'Waltz King', who composed nearly 400 new dance tunes, including the *Blue Danube* (1867). Today Strauss the Younger's house can be visited at Praterstrasse 54 (Tues–Thurs 2pm–6pm, Fri–Sun 10am–1pm). His statue graces the Stadtpark (see p 94) and his music is performed nightly in venues throughout the city (see The Best Arts & Entertainment, p 133).

Vienna p 48, bullet ❾). Schönberg famously developed 12-tone compositional technique, stretching the boundaries of 19th-century tonality to new dimensions. He founded the Second Viennese School of Music (along with fellow Viennese composers Alban Berg and Anton von Webern). Their music was not well received at the time, and Schönberg eventually moved to America. Today he is considered to be one of the most influential and distinguished composers of the 20th century. This fascinating modern center enables you to see the man behind the music—through his photos, brilliant artworks, reconstructed study, and homemade work tools (many from recycled materials)—and to listen to compositions by Schönberg, Webern, and Berg. ⏱ *45min. Zaunergasse 1–3 (take elevator in inner lobby area to the 1st floor, then ring on the doorbell).* ☎ *01 712 1888. www.schoenberg.at. €6 adults, €3 kids, €2.70 students. Mon–Fri 10am–5pm. Tram 1/2/D (Schwarzenbergplatz).*

Arnold Schönberg—a highly regarded teacher.

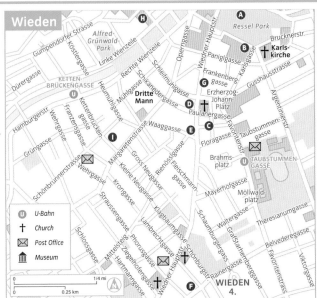

In **9A** ★ **Ressel Park**, a statue of the German romantic composer, Johannes Brahms, faces the Musikverein where he was once director. Brahms lived in nearby Karlsgasse, and was charmed by Vienna, calling it a 'village'. The Venetian baroque composer Antonio Vivaldi is buried at the **9B** ★ **Technische Universität** nearby. Richard Strauss, famed for his symphonic poems, lived at **9C** ★★★ **Mozartgasse** from 1919 to 1925. The Jugendstil 'Mozart Fountain' outside illustrates scenes from Mozart's opera *The Magic Flute*. German composer Christoph Willibald Gluck (director of Empress Maria Theresa's court orchestra) lived at **9D** ★ **Wiedner Hauptstrasse 32**. The Finnish composer Jean Sibelius lived at **9E** ★ **Waaggasse 1** from 1890 to 1891. He left Vienna having failed an audition to join the Vienna Philharmonic as a violinist. A plaque at **9F** ★ **Johann Strauss Gasse 4** marks the last home of Johann Strauss II. The opening bars of his celebrated *Blue Danube* waltz decorate the wall at number 10. Czech composer Antonín Dvořák frequented the former Hotel Goldenen Lamm at **9G** ★ **Wiedner Hauptstrasse 7**. The **9H** ★ **Theater an der Wien** (Linke Wienzeile 6) pays homage to Mozart with its *Papageno* statue (a reference to *The Magic Flute*). It premiered Beethoven's opera *Fidelio* in 1805. Franz Schubert died in 1828 at **9I** ★★ **Kettenbrückengasse 6**. Today it contains a small museum with a handful of poignant mementoes. ☎ 01 581 6730. www.wien museum.at. €2 adults, €1 kids, free on Sun. Fri–Sun 2pm–6pm.

9 ★★ **Wieden.** If you have time, explore the bohemian musicians' district of Wieden, just south of another great musical focal-point, the Musikverein (see p 13, bullet **7**). Here it is easy to see why Vienna is called the 'City of Music', as nearly every street bears a plaque to one musical genius or another. Start: Karlsplatz.

10 ★★★ kids **Haus der Musik.** In a city full of musical museums, this one is truly unique, focusing not only on Vienna's legacy of classical music but also on the science of sound and the listening process. Housed in the former residence of Otto Nicolai, founder of the celebrated Vienna Philharmonic Orchestra, it seems fitting that the first floor hosts the orchestra's archives (including sketches, letters, batons, posters, and scores by various composers including Bruckner, Brahms, and Richard Strauss), and a film of Vienna's illustrious New Year's Day concert. See p 43, bullet **4**.

11 ★★★ kids **Mozarthaus.** See p 12, bullet **4**.

12 ★★ **Central Cemetery.** Visit the final resting-places of many of the city's great musicians, including Beethoven, Brahms, Schubert, Schönberg, and all the Strausses at this vast cemetery which contains over 2½ million graves. Look out also for a monument to Mozart (who ended up in a paupers' grave in the evocatively overgrown St. Marx Cemetery). The cemetery's beautiful Jugendstil church was built in 1910 by Max Hegele, a pupil of Otto Wagner. A map near the entrance helps locate the celebrity

This elegant fountain representing Mozart's Magic Flute is tucked down a side street in Wieden.

graves. *Simmeringer Hauptstrasse 232–244.* ☎ *01 767 1507. Free admission. Nov–Feb 8am–5pm; Mar–Apr, Sept–Oct 7am–6pm; May–Aug 7am–7pm (last admission 30min before closing). Tram 6/71 (Zentralfriedhof).*

13 ★★ kids **Griechenbeisl.** Tuck into hearty Austrian cuisine in the cozy vaulted dining rooms (or shaded pavement terrace) of one of Vienna's oldest inns, located beside the ornate Greek Orthodox Church, and once frequented by Beethoven, Brahms, Schubert, and Mark Twain. *Fleischmarkt 11,* ☎ *01 533 1977. $$.*

14 ★★ **Musikverein.** A concert here marks the perfect ending to a musical day! See p 13, bullet **7**.

Kids' Vienna

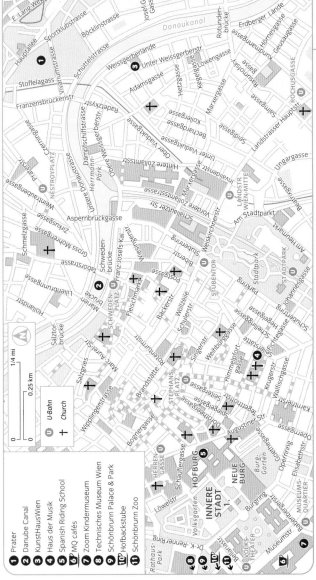

1. Prater
2. Danube Canal
3. KunstHausWien
4. Haus der Musik
5. Spanish Riding School
6. MQ cafés
7. Zoom Kindermuseum
8. Technisches Museum Wien
9. Schönbrunn Palace & Park
10. Hofbackstube
11. Schönbrunn Zoo

ienna may not seem the obvious choice for a family break but, believe me, my young family think it's quite the best city they've ever visited. *Fiakers* (horse-drawn carriages), tram rides, boat trips, the Prater ferris wheel, parks, playgrounds, and a host of child-friendly museums ensure kids of all ages will find plenty to amuse themselves.

1 ★★★ **kids** **Prater.** Kids young and old love the Riesenrad (big wheel), dodgem cars, and thrill-rides at the amusement park, as well as the green open spaces of the Prater for picnics, playgrounds, and sporting fun. *See p 96.*

2 ★★ **kids** **Danube Canal cruise.** *See p 100, bullet* **2**.

3 ★★★ **kids** **KunstHausWien.** Explore the curved and colorful world of the eccentric Austrian artist Friedensreich Hundertwasser. There's a special kids' tour and even a goodie bag for them to design their own KunstHaus (ask at reception). The café here is child-friendly too, with a lovely shaded patio garden. *See p 22, bullet* **4**.

4 ★★★ **kids** **Haus der Musik.** This eccentric venue describes itself as an 'interactive sound museum'. As well as the archives of the Vienna

KunstHausWien's café patio is ideal for family refreshments.

Philharmonic Orchestra, and a vivid portrayal of Vienna's classical composers, you can also explore the

The Prater amusement park—fun for all the family.

mechanics of sound and the experience of listening, through hands-on exhibits and instruments, state-of-the-art interactive toys, and touch screens. Test your hearing, compose your own waltz, record your own electronic CD and, best of all, conduct the Vienna Philharmonic using an electronic baton. The entire museum is like a giant musical theme park—especially enjoyable for older kids. ⏱ *1hr. Seilerstätter 30. ☎ 01 51648. www.hdm.at. €10 adults, €8.50 concessions, €5.50 kids (free under 3), €26 family ticket; combined ticket with Mozarthaus also available. Daily 10am–10pm. Make use of the late opening hours and go in the evenings. Tram 1/2/D/J (Oper).*

Fun and games at the KunstHausWien.

⑤ ★★ kids Spanish Riding School. The image of white Lipizzaner stallions performing dazzling dressage steps to waltz music is perhaps Vienna's most powerful marketing tool. A grand performance of these amazing equestrian gymnastics is an unforgettable treat. If you can't get tickets, attend a Privatissimum—a demonstration (in German and English) of their rigorous training routine. Alternatively, watch the dashingly uniformed riders perfect the art of classical horsemanship at the morning exercises. All events take place in the Hofburg's Winter Riding School, the world's oldest indoor riding school in a stately baroque style. *Michaelerplatz 1, Hofburg, Reitschulegasse 2. ☎ 01 533 9032–0 for Privatissimum and performance dates (most Fri 7pm, Sat 11am, Sun 11am except July–Aug). www.srs.at. Tickets: €22–165 (available online or from Michaelerplatz 1). Kids under 3 may not attend performances, but those aged 3–6 may attend free of charge if they sit on an adult's lap. Sit in the stalls or gallery I if possible). www.srs.at. Morning exercises: 10am–noon Tues–Sat Sept–June. Tickets: €12 adults, €6 kids (same day only, at Josefsplatz, Gate 2). U-Bahn 3 (Herrengasse).*

⑥ ★ kids MQ cafés. The MuseumsQuartier is crammed with eateries to suit all ages, tastes, and budgets. My two favorite lunch spots with kids are MQ Daily (☎ 01 522 4524, $) or the Dschungel Wien Café (☎ 01 522 0720, $) right outside Zoom Children's Museum (see below). If you eat al fresco, your offspring can run around outside and burn off some excess energy.

⑦ ★★★ kids Zoom Kindermuseum. This Children's Museum is brilliant. Designed exclusively for kids, it offers a wide variety of hands-on exhibitions and activities including the 'Ocean' play area (age 8months–6years); 'Let's get colorful' messy, arty workshops (age 3–12), and an exciting multimedia 'Zoom lab' (age 8–14). ⏱ *workshops last 1–11/2hr. Museumsplatz 1. ☎ 01 524 7908. Phone for times and prices. Reservations essential. Workshop staff speak German and English. www.kindermuseum.at. U-Bahn 2 (Museumsquartier).*

8 ★★★ kids **Technisches Museum Wien.** This huge Technical Museum is a little out of town, but easy to reach by U-Bahn. Kids love the old trams and planes, the hands-on technology displays, and interactive science experiments. There's even a special adventure area ('Das Mini') devoted to kids aged 2–6 (but also enjoyed by older kids) with activities such as changing the wheel on a car, running in a human-sized mouse wheel, and dressing up as fire-fighters. The café is reasonably priced and child-friendly too. ⏱ *2hr. Mariahilferstrasse 212.* ☎ *01 899 98–6000. www.technisches museum.at. €8.50 adults, €5 students & kids (free under 6), €7 senior citizens, €11 family ticket (1 adult plus 1 child) or €17 (2 adults plus 1 child), then €1.50 for each additional child. Mon–Fri 9am–6pm, Sat–Sun 10am–6pm. Tram 52/58 (Penzingerstrasse) or 10 (Johnstrasse/Linzerstrasse).*

Get lost in the maze at Schönbrunn!

9 ★★★ kids **Schönbrunn Palace and Park.** There's a huge amount for kids to do at the Schönbrunn Palace, including a puppet theater, a maze, a wacky playground, the zoo (see p 108, bullet **7**), and even a special Kindermuseum (Kids' Museum), where kids can experience something of the imperial way of life while playing with toys of the era, laying the table for a banquet, and dressing up in Habsburg costumes. *See p 104.* ⏱ *1–4hr. Kindermuseum.* ☎ *01 811 13-239. www.kinder.schoenbrunn.at. €6.50 adults, €5 concessions, €4.90 kids (3–18), €10.50/€17 family. Sat–Sun 10am–5pm (last admission 4pm), also daily 10am–5pm during school vacations. U-Bahn 4 (Schönbrunn).*

The Kindermuseum—just for kids.

10 ★★ kids **Hofbackstube— Apple Strudel Show.** Watch confectioners making traditional apple strudel in the old-fashioned 'Court Bakery', then eat one, piping hot, straight from the oven. ⏱ *1hr. Kavalierstrakt 52.* ☎ *01 811 13–239. www.schoenbrunn.at. €3.90. Hourly demonstrations daily 10am–5pm, mid-Mar–Oct. U-Bahn 4 (Schloss Schönbrunn).*

11 ★★★ kids **Schönbrunn Zoo.** See p 108, bullet **7**.

The Best Special-Interest Tours

Jewish Vienna

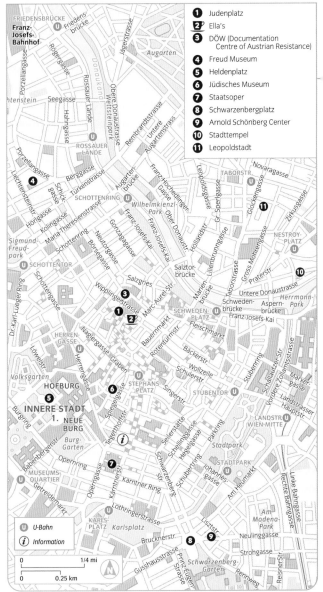

1. Judenplatz
2. Ella's
3. DÖW (Documentation Centre of Austrian Resistance)
4. Freud Museum
5. Heldenplatz
6. Jüdisches Museum
7. Staatsoper
8. Schwarzenbergplatz
9. Arnold Schönberg Center
10. Stadttempel
11. Leopoldstadt

U U-Bahn
ⓘ Information

0   1/4 mi
0   0.25 km

'It is impossible to imagine what it means for one-sixth of the population to be made pariahs overnight, deprived of all human rights . . .' wrote a wartime correspondent in 1938, describing the plight of Viennese Jews. Jews have been persecuted in this city on more than one occasion, despite their outstanding contribution to the arts, science, and politics. Their remarkable story is intrinsic to the history of Vienna.

1 ★★ **Judenplatz.** This square marks the heart of the medieval Jewish ghetto. The first expulsion of Vienna's Jews took place in 1421. You can learn more about the ghetto during that period at the Judenplatz Museum, and visit the remains of one of Europe's largest medieval synagogues, excavated in 1995. In the square, I love the stark poignancy of the modern stone monument devoted to the Holocaust. Designed by British sculptress Rachel Whitbread, and erected in 2000, it resembles an inside-out library of nameless books lined up on bookshelves with their spines facing inwards, symbolizing the many stories of the victims left untold. ⏱ *30min. Judenplatz. Museum: Judenplatz 8.* ☎ *01 535 0431. www.jmw.at. €4 adults, €2.50 concessions. Sun–Thurs 10am–6pm, Fri 10am–2pm. U-Bahn U1/3 (Stephansplatz).*

2 **Ella's.** This bright, modern café-restaurant serves a superb range of coffee, and a mouth-watering menu of 'Mediterranean soul food' on its sunny terrace. The lemon risotto with *haloumi* is especially tasty. *Judenplatz 9-10.* ☎ *01 535 1577. $–$$.*

3 ★★★ **Documentation Center of Austrian Resistance (DÖW).** Fascinating but inevitably harrowing, this small museum documents the early history of National Socialism and the persecution of its opponents. ⏱ *1hr. Altes Rathaus, Wipplingerstrasse 8.* ☎ *01 228 9469 0319. www.doew.at. Free. Mon–Fri 9am–5pm (7pm Thurs). U-Bahn 1/3 (Stephansplatz).*

4 ★ **Freud Museum.** *See p 73, bullet* **8**.

5 ★★ **Heldenplatz.** 'Heroes Square', in front of the Neue Burg

Austria's Tomb of the Unknown Soldier—Castle Gate at Heldenplatz.

LAVRVM. MILITIBVS. LAVRO. DIGNIS. MDCCCCXV

(see p 60, bullet ⑤) was built by the Habsburgs as a symbol of imperial strength. But it will go down in history as the scene of Hitler's 1938 fateful speech to thousands of cheering Austrians when he announced the infamous *Anschluss* (Annexation), assimilating Austria into the Third Reich. By 1945, Heldenplatz had been ploughed up to plant vegetables to feed Vienna's suffering citizens. Since 1955, the Burgtor (Castle Gate) on the south-western side of the square has served as Austria's Tomb of the Unknown Soldier. ⏱ *15min. Heldenplatz. Tram 1/2/D/J (Burgring).*

⑥ ★★ **Jüdisches Museum.** The world's first Jewish Museum opened in Vienna in 1895, but the exhibits were confiscated by the Nazis in 1938. Today's museum opened in 1993 and contains an important collection of Judaica and an extraordinary fresco-like 'Installation of Remembrance'. ⏱ *45min. Dorotheergasse 11. ☎ 01 535 0431. www. jmw.at. Sun–Fri 10am–6pm. €6.50 adults, €4 concessions (free under 10). U-Bahn 1/3 (Stephansplatz).*

⑦ ★★★ **Staatsoper.** The State Opera has always attracted top international conductors, including Richard Strauss, Herbert von Karajan, and Claudio Abbado. Its most controversial appointment was Jewish-born Gustav Mahler, who directed the opera-house for 10 years from 1897 to 1907. As this was an 'imperial' post and thus barred to Jews under Austro-Hungarian law, Mahler converted to Catholicism. During his tenure, Mahler made radical changes to operatic conventions, such as dimming audience lighting during the performance, shortening intervals, and seating late arrivals only during intermissions—now all standard practices worldwide. *See p 38, bullet ⑦.*

⑧ ★ **Schwarzenbergplatz.** This grandiose square was the seat of the military government during World War II, when it was known as 'Stalinplatz' and used for military parades. The giant bronze Russen Heldendenkmal (Russian Heroes Memorial) was created in 1945. Weighing 15 tons, it was made out of hundreds of melted-down busts of Hitler. *Schwarzenbergplatz. Tram 1/2/D (Schwarzenbergplatz).*

⑨ ★★ **Arnold Schönberg Center.** This archive center provides a unique insight into the life and

Image of Mahler in the Leopold Museum.

Kristallnacht

Many historians date the beginning of the Holocaust to November 9, 1938, when the Nazi government launched a vicious attack on the Jewish community throughout Germany and Austria. This was particularly ruthless in Vienna, where the Jewish population was around 200,000 (over 10% of the city's inhabitants). Stormtroopers torched 42 of Vienna's 43 synagogues, looted shops and businesses, and ransacked homes. The event became known as *Kristallnacht*—the 'Night of Glass'—because of the shattered glass found on the pavements outside Jewish premises the following day.

music of the Jewish composer, who is now recognized as a profound influence on modern classical music. Initially, however, Schönberg's innovative 12-tone compositions received a poor reception in Vienna and in 1933, perturbed by the rise of National Socialism, he emigrated to America. *See p 38, bullet* **8**.

10 ★ **Stadttempel.** The City Synagogue, designed in 1826 by the renowned local architect Kornhäusel, was the only Viennese synagogue to survive Kristallnacht (see below), thanks largely to its concealed façade. Today it remains at the heart of Vienna's Jewish community. Its impressive elliptical interior features a blue dome, marble columns, and a three-tiered gallery. *Seitenstettengasse 2–4.* ☎ *01 531 04–0. €3 adults, €2 concessions. Guided tours only: 11.30am and 2pm, Mon–Thurs (except Jewish holidays). Bring your passport for ID and arrive 15 minutes beforehand. U-Bahn 1/4 (Schwedenplatz).*

11 ★ **Leopoldstadt.** The city's ancient Jewish district was created north of the Danube Canal in the Leopoldstadt quarter, following an imperial decree in 1624 that Jews had to live outside the city walls.

Half a century later, Emperor Leopold I expelled all Jews from Vienna, and the great synagogue was converted into the Church of St. Leopold. Today, parts of Leopoldstadt retain a Jewish atmosphere, with synagogues, kosher shops, and Jewish schools. Four slim columns (at Tempelgasse 5) mark the location of the former Great Temple, destroyed on Kristallnacht. *U-Bahn 1 (Nestroyplatz).*

These four columns mark the site of Leopoldstadt's former Great Temple.

'The Third Man' in Vienna

Symbol	Legend		
U	U-Bahn	**1**	Third Man Private Collection
†	Church	**2**	Beethovenplatz
✉	Post Office	**3**	Sewers
🎭	Theater	**4**	Imperial, Bristol & Sacher Hotels
🏛	Museum	**5**	Café Mozart
···	Walking Path	**6**	Schreyvogelgasse 8
		7	Prater - Riesenrad

The classic 1949 thriller *The Third Man* is an undisputed masterpiece of British film noir. Scripted by Graham Greene and directed by Carol Reed, it features a legendary performance by Orson Welles, who plays the central character Harry Lime. A multi-layered film of friendship and betrayal, it provides a unique and authentic testimony of life in the bombed-out ruins of post-World-War-II Vienna.

1 ★★ Third Man Private Collection. Any fan of the cult movie should visit this tiny museum, which provides a fascinating insight into the making of *The Third Man*. ⏱ 45min. Pressgasse 25. ☎ 01 586 4872. www.3mpc.net. €7.50 adults, €6 concessions, €5 kids (10–16). Sat 2pm–6pm (also Tues 6pm–8pm by prior arrangement). U-Bahn 4 (Kettenbrückengasse).

2 ★ Beethovenplatz. The Beethoven statue here is featured at the start of the movie. Note the advertising kiosk nearby. During police raids, black-market crooks would disappear into such kiosks, and then down a manhole into the sewers. *Beethovenplatz. U-Bahn 4 (Stadtpark).*

3 ★★ kids Sewers. The climax of the movie takes place in the sewers, when Lime is eventually cornered by police and shot dead. The police enter the sewer system via a steel hatch (in Friedrichstrasse). This also marks the start of the city's thrilling sewer tour. ⏱ 1hr. *Karlsplatz-*

Graham Greene's favorite café.

Esperantopark. ☎ *01 4000 3033. €7 adults, €5.50 concessions (minimum age 12). May–Oct, Thurs–Sun 10am–10pm (tours every hour). U-Bahn 1/2/4 (Karlsplatz).*

❹ ★ Imperial, Bristol & Sacher Hotels. In 1945 for ten years, Vienna was divided into international zones by the occupying Allied powers. The centre was an 'international' sector, with the American Intelligence based at Hotel Bristol, the Russians at the Imperial, and the British at the Sacher—where Martins stays in the film, and where Greene conceived the film from his intelligence cronies in the bar, including his boss the famous KGB double agent Kim Philby, the inspiration for Harry Lime. *Kärtner Ring & Philharmonikerstrasse. Tram 1/2/D/J (Oper).*

❺ Café Mozart. Inspired by Greene's favorite café, musician Anton Karas composed a 'Café Mozart Waltz' for the movie. The café scenes were actually shot in a mocked-up set near the Kapuzinerkirche (Capuchin Church), because the square was still full of wartime rubble in 1948. Round the corner is Harry's house, Palais Palavincini (in Josephsplatz). *Albertinaplatz 2.* ☎ *01 241 00–0. $-$$. Tram 1/2/D/J (Oper).*

❻ ★ Schreyvogelgasse 8. This is the site of one of the most dramatic moments in the movie when Harry emerges from the shadows, very much alive, in the doorway here on the Mölker Bastei. *Schreyvogelgasse 8. U-Bahn 2 (Schottentor).*

❼ ★★★ kids Prater—Riesenrad. Ride on the 200ft Riesenrad ferris wheel, one of Vienna's most famous landmarks, immortalized in the movie as the pivotal scene when Martins and Lime eventually meet and Martins learns the awful truth about his friend. *See p 98, bullet* ❹.

A cult address—Schreyvogelgasse 8.

Best Churches

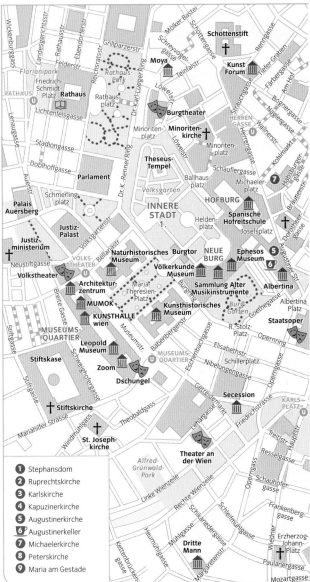

1 Stephansdom
2 Ruprechtskirche
3 Karlskirche
4 Kapuzinerkirche
5 Augustinerkirche
6 Augustinerkeller
7 Michaelerkirche
8 Peterskirche
9 Maria am Gestade

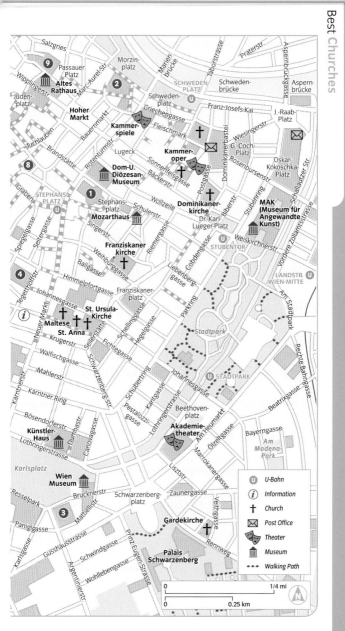

0   1/4 mi

0   0.25 km

I love Viennese churches. They showcase the city's best architecture, and they also contain some of Vienna's finest artworks and treasures. What's more, they provide a fascinating historical record of the customs, traditions, and extraordinary burial rituals of the Viennese over the centuries.

1 ★★★ **Stephansdom.** There has been a church in Stephansplatz for over 800 years, but all that remains of the original 13th-century Romanesque building is the *Riesentor* (Giants' Doorway) and the twin towers at the main entrance. The glorious Gothic nave, choir, and side-chapels date from the 14th and 15th centuries (some baroque chapels were added later). After extensive damage at the end of World War II, the citizens of Vienna financed the rebuilding of the cathedral as a symbol of national solidarity after the horrors of the Nazi regime. *See p 11, bullet* **3**.

2 ★★★ **Ruprechtskirche.** *See p 65, bullet* **11**.

3 ★★★ **Karlskirche.** Vienna's most impressive baroque church, and its most important sacred building after the Stephansdom. Visit it at sunset to see the magnificent dome at its best. *See p 67, bullet* **5**.

The Stephansdom's intricately tiled roof is a sight to behold.

This angel on the façade of Karlskirche represents the New Testament.

4 ★★★ **Kapuzinerkirche.** The Church of Capuchin Friars resembles a country church, charming in its simplicity. Its main appeal is the spine-chilling *Kaisergruft* (Imperial Burial Vault), which served as the Habsburgs' burial place for over 350 years—12 emperors and 19 empresses lie here in elaborate sarcophagi. A rather gruesome Habsburg mortuary ritual was to inter the hearts of the imperial family separately in the crypt of the Augustinerkirche (see below), while the intestines were placed in copper urns in the catacombs beneath the Stephansdom. ⏱ *45min. Tegethoffstrasse 2.* ☎ *01 512 6853–16. www.kaisergruft.at. €4 adults, €3 concessions, €1.50 kids, €9 family. 10am–6pm (last admission 5.40pm). Tram D/J/1/2 (Oper).*

5 ★ **Augustinerkirche.** The former Court Church has witnessed numerous imperial weddings over the centuries, including Marie Louise's marriage to Napoleon in 1810 and that of Franz Joseph I to Sisi in 1854. Besides a stunning Gothic interior, it is renowned for the pyramidal tomb of Maria Christina by the Italian neoclassical sculptor Antonio Canova. Its crypt houses 54 silver casks containing the hearts of the Habsburgs (see above). ⏱ *20min. Augustinerstrasse 3 (entrance on Josefsplatz).* ☎ *01 533 7090. www.augustiner kirche.at. Free admission. Open 8am–6pm. U3 (Herrengasse).*

This lion guards Maria Christina's tomb in Augustinerkirche.

6 **Augustinerkeller.** Head here for hearty Austrian specialties washed down by local wines or beer on tap, in a snug, brick-vaulted bar set in former monastery cellars. Jolly live music plays every evening from 6.30pm. *Augustinerstrasse 1.* ☎ *01 533 1026. $$.*

7 ★ **Michaelerkirche.** St. Michael's Church is a hotchpotch of

Hard to believe the beautiful Maria am Gestade was once used as an arsenal and stables.

styles from Romanesque to baroque. Its main point of interest is the crypt. During the 17th and 18th centuries, parishioners were usually buried beneath their church—well-preserved corpses are still visible in open coffins. ⏱ *1hr (including 40min tour of crypt). Michaelerplatz.* ☎ *0650 533 8003. www.michaeler gruft.at. €5. Mon, Tues, Thurs–Sat 11am, 1.30pm, Wed 11am (Easter–Nov), by appointment only in winter. U-Bahn 3 (Herrengasse).*

8 ★★ **Peterskirche.** See p 63, bullet **5**.

9 ★★★ **Maria am Gestade.** 'St. Mary on the Riverbank'—my favorite church—is a jewel of Gothic architecture, with slender vaults, buttresses, and a canopied porch. Built on a steep bank, it originally overlooked the Danube. The main door resembles a ship's prow, and its delicate seven-sided filigree tower served as a landmark for boatmen approaching the city. Don't miss the Gothic stained glass in the choir inside. More would have survived, had Napoleon's troops not used the church as an arsenal and stables during their occupation of Vienna in 1809. ⏱ *20min. Salvatorgasse 12.* ☎ *01 533 9594–0. www.maria-am-gestade.redemptoristen.at. 8am–3pm. U-Bahn 1/4 (Schwedenplatz).*

The **Ringstrasse**

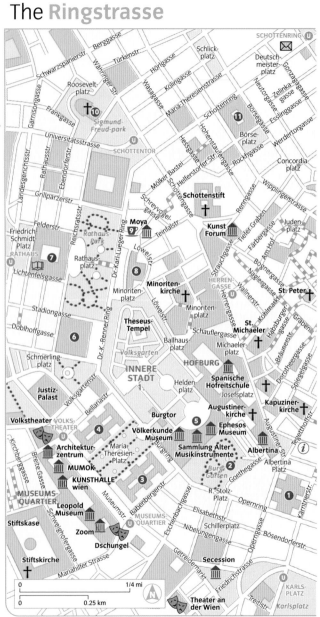

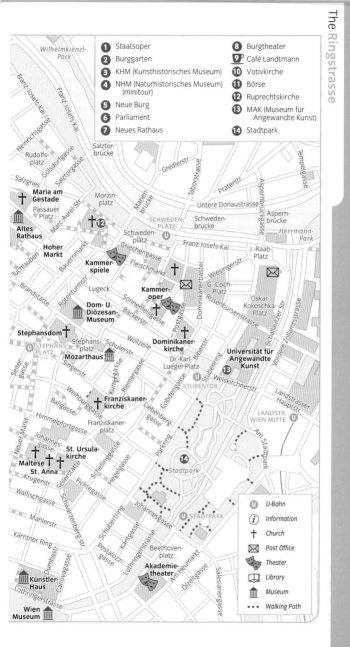

1 Staatsoper
2 Burggarten
3 KHM (Kunsthistorisches Museum)
4 NHM (Naturhistorisches Museum) (minitour)
5 Neue Burg
6 Parliament
7 Neues Rathaus
8 Burgtheater
9 Café Landtmann
10 Votivkirche
11 Börse
12 Ruprechtskirche
13 MAK (Museum für Angewandte Kunst)
14 Stadtpark

U U-Bahn
i Information
† Church
✉ Post Office
🎭 Theater
📖 Library
🏛 Museum
••• Walking Path

With the demolition of the old city walls and the construction of the magnificent Ringstrasse, Emperor Franz Josef ushered in a new era of grandeur in his expansion of the inner city in the 19th century. Today this circular boulevard still separates the historic city center from the suburbs. It is as grand now as it was then, and it's fun and easy to explore by tram. Just hop aboard tram 1 or 2 for a whistle-stop tour.

1 ★★★ Staatsoper. The world-famous State Opera was the first of the monumental new public buildings on the Ringstrasse. It was built in the Historicist (neo-Renaissance) style in 1861–9 by architects Null and Sicardsburg. Harsh criticism from the public, who thought the opera-house looked like a railway station, drove Null to commit suicide and, a few weeks later—before the project was completed—a distressed Sicardsburg died from a heart attack. The building was badly damaged in World War II. Ironically, the Viennese were keen to restore it to its former glory after the war, and the opera-house finally reopened in 1955 with a triumphant performance of Beethoven's *Fidelio*. **See p 18, bullet 9.**

This sculpture of King Thutmosis III at the KHM dates from around 1460BC.

2 ★★ kids Burggarten. With its duck pond, butterfly house, fine statuary, and magnificent Jugendstil glasshouse (see p 35, bullet 10), this beautiful English-style park was originally reserved for the emperor's family. It was opened to the public in 1919 and is now one of the city's most popular open spaces. *Burgring. Daily 6am–10pm. Tram 1/2/D/J (Burgring).*

3 ★★★ Kunsthistorisches Museum (KHM). See p 18, bullet 8.

The celebrated Staatsoper.

④ ★★★ kids Naturhistorisches Museum (NHM). Trace the history of the planet and admire a multiplicity of animal species on display at the Natural History Museum. This huge museum is a mirror-image of the grand Renaissance-style Kunsthistorisches Museum on the opposite side of the Ringstrasse. Within its majestic display halls lies a bewildering array of archeological, anthropological, mineralogical, zoological, and geological specimens.

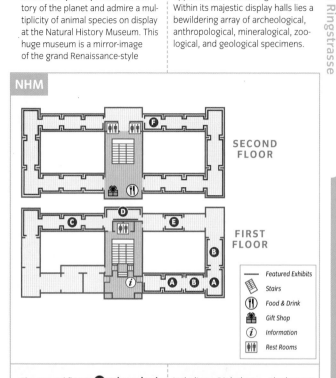

NHM

SECOND FLOOR

FIRST FLOOR

— Featured Exhibits
📄 Stairs
🍴 Food & Drink
🎁 Gift Shop
ⓘ Information
🚻 Rest Rooms

The ground floor's **④A mineralogical collection** contains over a thousand different mineral specimens (Halls I–III) and one of Europe's most valuable gem collections (Hall IV). Look out for the valuable bouquet of jewels given by Maria Theresa to her husband. **④B Halls V–VI** display hundreds of meteorites and moon-rocks, and show how the earth is affected by day, night, the changing seasons, ocean currents, and ozone layers. The **④C prehistory section** contains the world's largest display of human skulls. Kids love the mezzanine floor and especially **④D Room 10** with its massive dinosaur skeletons, including a Diplodocus—the longest terrestrial vertebrate that has ever lived at 90ft (27m). In **④E Room VII,** a fossil of the **world's largest spider** is not for the squeamish. The first floor covers ecology, with room after room of every type of **④F stuffed animal** imaginable, including numerous species now extremely endangered or extinct. 🕐 *2–3 hr. Maria Theresien-Platz, Burgring 7.* ☎ *01 521 77-0. www.nhm-wien.ac.at. €8 adults, €6 concessions, €3.50 kids (free under 5), €16–€10 family card. Wed–Mon 9am–6.30pm (until 9pm Wed). Tram D/J/1/2 (Dr-Karl-Renner Ring, Naturhistorisches Museum).*

Skeleton of a Tryceratops head, Natural History Museum.

5 ★ **Neue Burg.** Emperor Franz Joseph had plans for two crescent-shaped buildings in his Neue Burg (New Castle), but only one was completed before the Habsburg Empire collapsed in 1918. Today, this vast edifice, with its colonnaded façade, houses several museums. The Ephesus Museum (Greek and Roman antiquities), the Imperial Armory (Europe's most comprehensive weaponry collection), and the Old Musical Instruments Collection (see p 37, bullet **4**) are all worth a visit. ⏱ *1–2hr. Heldenplatz.* ☎ *01 525 24–0. www.khm.at. Combined admission for all three museums: €8 adults, €6 concessions, €3 kids, €16 family, €3 audio guide. Wed–Mon 10am–6pm. Tram 1/2/D/J (Burgring).*

6 ★ **Parliament.** The Greek-style Parliament building makes a dignified landmark with its classical columns and statues of Greek philosophers. The first Austrian Republic was proclaimed from the Parliament steps in October 1918. *Dr-Karl-Renner-Ring 3. Free admission. Mon–Fri 7am–7pm. Tram D/J/1/2 (Dr-Karl-Renner Ring, Naturhistorisches Museum).*

7 ★★ **kids Neues Rathaus.** Festooned with ornamental tracery, loggias, and spires, the neo-Gothic New Town Hall is the showiest building on the Ringstrasse. Atop the main tower is a statue of a knight holding a lance, affectionately called the *Rathausmann*. There is a flag attached to the lance, with a star at the top, which also serves as a lightning conductor. The large square in front of the town hall always seems to have some sort of festivity: open-air cinema in summer; ice-skating in winter; and—my favorite—the Christmas market (Christkindlmarkt). *Rathausplatz.* ☎ *01 52550. Guided tours Mon, Wed, Fri 1pm. Free admission. U-Bahn 2 (Rathaus).*

8 ★★ **Burgtheater.** The most prestigious theater venue in the German-speaking world is known not only for drama but also for its grand staircases and frescoes by Gustav Klimt. Constructed in Italian Renaissance style in 1888, the theater was rebuilt following severe damage during World War II. *Dr-Karl-Lueger-Ring 2.* ☎ *01 514 444 140. www.burg theater.at. Tours daily 3pm (also 2pm July–Aug). Tram D/1/2 (Burgtheater).*

9 **Café Landtmann.** Ignore the ugly modern sun-terrace outside and step indoors to a *fin-de-siècle* wonderland of ornate mirrors and paneled wood. Coffee and cake here is a quintessential experience. No wonder this was Freud's favorite café. *Dr-Karl-Lueger-Ring 4.* ☎ *01 24100. $$.*

10 ★ **Votivkirche.** *See p 72, bullet* **6**.

11 ★ **Börse.** *See p 72, bullet* **7**.

12 ★★★ **Ruprechtskirche.** *See p 65, bullet* **11**.

13 ★★ **Museum für Angewandte Kunst (MAK).** *See p 12, bullet* **5**.

14 ★★ **kids Stadtpark.** *See p 94.* ●

Stephansdom **District**

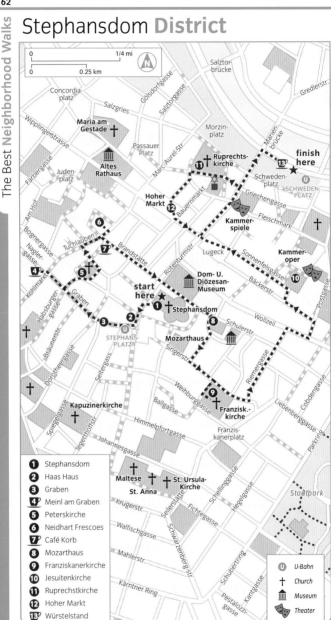

1 Stephansdom
2 Haas Haus
3 Graben
4 Meinl am Graben
5 Peterskirche
6 Neidhart Frescoes
7 Café Korb
8 Mozarthaus
9 Franziskanerkirche
10 Jesuitenkirche
11 Ruprechstkirche
12 Hoher Markt
13 Würstelstand

U U-Bahn
† Church
▥ Museum
🎭 Theater

This is a walk to suit the whole family. It takes you right to the historic heart of Vienna, to the foundations of ancient Roman Vindobona, and to some of the city's oldest inns and churches. Explore the atmospheric maze of medieval alleyways surrounding Stephansdom, visit the Mozarthaus, and enjoy the best apple strudel in town—as well as the smart shops of the Graben—as well as the best apple strudel in town.

❶ ★★★ Stephansdom. *See p 11, bullet* ❸.

❷ ★★ Haas Haus. Created by Hans Hollein in the 1980s, this curvaceous building of polished granite, concrete, and glass, which houses a boutique hotel on the 6th and 7th floor, is one of Vienna's most controversial pieces of modern architecture. Love it or hate it, it offers tremendous views of the Stephansdom from the rooftop bar (6th floor) and restaurant (7th floor). *Stock-im-Eisenplatz. U-Bahn 1/3 (Stephansplatz).*

❸ ★★ Graben. This broad, pedestrianized shopping street was once the town moat, hence the name Graben (ditch). It later became a marketplace and is now one of the city's finest boulevards. All the buildings date from the baroque, 19th-century or Belle Époque eras, and many still bear their K.u.K. (Kaiserlich und Königlich—Imperial and Royal) warrant. The exuberant baroque Pestsäule (Plague Column) in the middle of the street was erected to commemorate Vienna's deliverance from the plague of 1679. *Graben. U-Bahn 1/3 (Stephansplatz).*

The Plague Column on the Graben.

❹ ★★★ Meinl am Graben. Join shoppers on the sun-terrace for coffee and cake at Vienna's most elegant café-delicatessen. At the junction of two fashionable shopping streets, it's a prime spot for people-watching (see p 63). *Kohlmarkt 1.* ☎ *01 532 3334. $–$$$.*

❺ ★★ Peterskirche. St. Peter's is my favorite baroque church. Full of pomp and grandeur, yet intimate at the same time, its superb acoustics make it a marvelous concert venue. I love the graceful oval nave and the pews, each decorated with three carved angels' heads, but the artistic *pièce de résistance* is undoubtedly the spectacular fresco on the domed ceiling entitled *The Martyrdom of St. Sebastian*, by Michael Rottmayr. 🕐 *30min. Petersplatz.* ☎ *01 533 6433. Mon–Fri 7am–7pm, Sat–Sun 8am–8pm. Occasional free concerts (including daily organ recitals at 3pm in summer). U-Bahn 1/3 (Stephansplatz).*

6 ★★ **Neidhart Frescoes.** One of Vienna's best-kept secrets, these richly colored wall paintings are the oldest secular frescoes in the city. They were commissioned by a cloth merchant around the year 1407. Their scenes of love and revelry (depicting the four seasons) were inspired by the songs of the lyrical poet Neidhart von Reuenthal, who revived the courtly love song in the early Middle Ages. Fun and frivolous, they give a lively and humorous insight into medieval life. ⏱ *30min. Tuchlauben 19.* ☎ *01 535 9065. www.wienmuseum.at. €2 adults, €1 concessions, kids, free admission on Sun. Tues 10am–1pm, 2pm–6pm, Fri–Sun 2pm–6pm. U-Bahn 1/3 (Stephansplatz).*

The fez-wearing Meinl Moor—the symbol of Vienna's finest deli and a reminder of the city's Turkish coffee origins.

7 ★★★ **Café Korb.** The main reason to take a break here is to try the scrumptious *Apfelstrudel* (apple strudel)—quite the best I've tasted. The pavement terrace with its tiny fountain is a pleasant place to sit and write postcards, or to catch up with the news from the pile of international newspapers. *Brandstätte 9.* ☎ *01 533 7215. $–$$.*

Peterskirche is hidden just off the Graben.

8 ★★★ **kids Mozarthaus.** It is easy to imagine Mozart living in this apartment for four years with his young family, a dog, and a songbird, thanks to the paintings, estate deeds, letters, death mask, manuscripts, and musical instruments on display. *See p 12, bullet* **4**.

9 ★ **Franziskanerkirche.** The Franciscan Church is the only church in Vienna with a Renaissance façade. The interior is a striking blend of Gothic and northern Renaissance style, with numerous later baroque features. The square outside contains a copy of an 18th-century Moses Fountain (the original was melted down by the Nazis) and the charming pint-sized Kleines Café. ⏱ *20min. Franziskanerplatz.* ☎ *01 512 4578. Daily 8am–6pm. U-Bahn 1/3 (Stephansplatz).*

10 ★ **Jesuitenkirche.** The Jesuit Church, built in 1627, is one of the city's finest baroque churches, decked in a profusion of pink granite and gilt. The Italian *tromp-l'oeil* artist Andrea Pozzo remodeled the interior in the early 18th century, adding its impressive frescoes and a false 'dome' on a flat part of the ceiling. Stand in the nave on the spot marked with a white stone to see this ingenious illusion. ⏱ 20min. Dr Ignaz Seipel-Platz. ☎ 01 512 5232. Mon–Fri 8am–6pm, Sat–Sun 8am–7pm. U-Bahn 3 (Stubentor).

⓫ ★★★ Ruprechtskirche. I love the simplicity of this tiny ivy-clad Romanesque church—Vienna's oldest. Set in a quiet, cobbled square off the beaten tourist track, it is dedicated to St. Rupert, the patron saint of salt merchants and the first Bishop of Salzburg. Salt barges would once have passed by this church on the banks of the Danube. A statue of St. Rupert, clutching a barrel of salt, can be found half-hidden among bushes beside the church. Visit in the morning when the ancient stained-glass windows bathe the interior in brightly colored light. ⏱ 20min. Ruprechtsplatz. ☎ 01 535 6003. Mon, Wed, Fri 10am–noon, Tues, Thurs 2–4pm, Fri 9pm–midnight. Free admission. U-Bahn 1/4 (Schwedenplatz).

⓬ ★★★ Hoher Markt. Most visitors head towards Vienna's oldest square, site of a medieval fish-market, to see the splendid Jugendstil clock known as the Ankeruhr. Every hour on the hour, historical figures

You're never far from a Wuerstelstand in Vienna.

The Anker clock at Hoher Markt.

(including the Roman emperor Marcus Aurelius, Duke Rudolf IV, and Joseph Haydn) parade across the golden clock-face. It's best viewed at noon, when all the figures emerge. Beneath the square, you can see the city's best-preserved Roman remains in the small but fascinating **Römermuseum**, where the legionary fortress of Vindobona stood nearly 2,000 years ago. ⏱ 45min. Hoher Markt 3. ☎ 01 535 5606. www.wienmuseum.at. €4 adults, €3 concessions (OAPs, VCs, kids), free under 6, €10 family, free Sun. Tues–Sun 9am–6pm. U-Bahn 1/3 (Stephansplatz).

⓭ ★ kids Würstelstand. Night owls meet early birds here (open 8am–4am) for coffee, refreshments, or a snack—sausages, kebabs, pizza and so on. After an evening partying in the bars of the nearby 'Bermuda Triangle' night zone (around Rotenturmstrasse), I recommend the hearty Käsekrainer sausages, made with grilled meat and cheese. Schwedenplatz. No phone. $.

The **Belvedere**

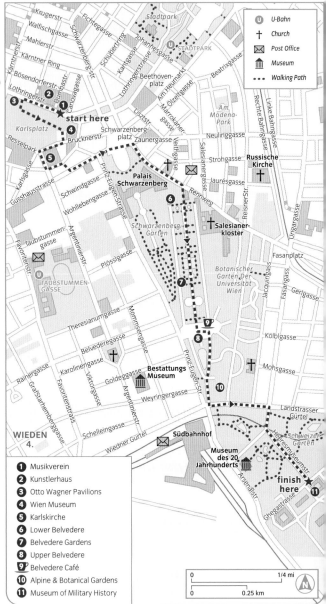

Legend:
- Ⓤ U-Bahn
- ✝ Church
- ✉ Post Office
- 🏛 Museum
- ··· Walking Path

Map labels:

Krugerstr, Walfischgasse, Mahlerstr, Kärntnerstr, Kärntner Ring, Bösendorferstr, Lothringerstr, Canovagasse, Dumbastr, Fichtegasse, Schwarzenbergstr, Schubertring, Karlsgasse, Lothringerstrasse, Johannesgasse, Beethovenplatz, Am Heumarkt, Beatrixgasse, Ölzeltgasse, Marrokaner gasse, Liststr, Schwarzenberg-platz, Zaunergasse, Veithgasse, Salesianergasse, Neulinggasse, Strohgasse, Jaurésgasse, Reisnerstr, Rechte Bahngasse, Linke Bahngasse, Am Modena-Park, Ungargasse, Fasanplatz, Jacquingasse, Fasangasse, Gerlgasse, Kölblgasse, Mohsgasse, Landstrasser Gürtel, Ghegastrasse, Arsenalstr, Heeresmuseumstr, Schweizer Garten, Wiedner Gürtel, Schelleingasse, Weyringergasse, Goldeggasse, Viktorgasse, Argentinierstr, Favoritenstr, Karolinengasse, Rainergasse, Grafstarhenbergstrass, Belvederegasse, Theresianumgasse, Mommsengasse, Plösslgasse, Taubstummengasse, Argentinierstr, Wohllebengasse, Schwindgasse, Prinz-Eugen-Strasse, Gusshausstrasse, Resselpark, Karlsgasse, Brucknerstr, Rennweg

Stadtpark, STADTPARK, Russische Kirche, Palais Schwarzenberg, Schwarzenberg-Garten, Salesianer-kloster, Botanischer Garten Der Universität Wien, TAUBSTUMMEN-GASSE, WIEDEN 4., Bestattungs Museum, Südbahnhof, Museum des 20 Jahrhunderts

start here

finish here

1. Musikverein
2. Kunstlerhaus
3. Otto Wagner Pavilions
4. Wien Museum
5. Karlskirche
6. Lower Belvedere
7. Belvedere Gardens
8. Upper Belvedere
9. Belvedere Café
10. Alpine & Botanical Gardens
11. Museum of Military History

| 0 | | 1/4 mi |
| 0 | | 0.25 km |

I love the extravagance of the Belvedere district. Vienna's aristocracy built their lavish summer residences in the countryside here during the 18th and 19th centuries. Today, this charming district of palaces and parks takes life at a sedate pace, despite being so close to the city center.

1 ★★ **Musikverein.** *See p 13, bullet* **7**.

2 ★ **Kunstlerhaus.** The Artists' House was commissioned in 1868 by the Austrian Artists' Association as an exhibition hall for its members, and is still a popular venue for temporary exhibitions. Its architecture is a typical example of the Ringstrasse's pompous historical style. *Karlsplatz 5.* ☎ *01 587 9663. www.k-haus.at. Daily 10am–6pm (Thurs until 9pm). U-Bahn 1/2/4 (Karlsplatz).*

3 ★★ **Otto Wagner Pavilions.** *See p 33, bullet* **2**.

4 ★★★ **Wien Museum.** *See p 16, bullet* **1**.

5 ★★★ **Karlskirche.** The colossal dome of this high-baroque church dominates the square of Karlsplatz on which it stands. Designed in 1716 by Fischer von Erlach, the Karlskirche showcases the work of the most important

architects and artists of the time. It was originally commissioned by Emperor Karl VI, who made a solemn vow to build a great church during a virulent outbreak of plague in 1713. It is dedicated to the emperor's namesake, St. Carlo Borromeo, the patron saint of plagues. Its remarkable architectural complexity pays homage to St. Peter's Basilica in Rome, to the Roman emperors Augustus and Trajan, and to the Temple of Solomon in Jerusalem. St. Carlo sits happily on top of the portico alongside statues of Religion, Mercy, Repentance, and Piety, flanked by two angels representing the Old and New Testaments. The triumphal pillars (modeled on Trajan's Column in Rome and crowned by imperial eagles) show scenes from Borromeo's life. Unlike some baroque churches, the oval interior is light and airy, and its decoration is agreeably restrained. The frescoes by Michael Rottmayr are especially

It's hard to beat Karlskirche for Baroque architectural extravagance.

fine. *Karlsplatz.* ☎ *01 504 6187. www.karlskirche.at. €6 adults, €4 students & kids (free under 10). Open Mon–Sat 9am–12.30pm, 1–6pm, Sun 1–6pm. Holy Mass Mon–Sat 6pm, Sun 11am & 6pm. U-Bahn 1/2/4 (Karlsplatz).*

⑥ ★ Lower Belvedere. Prince Eugene of Savoy, the most important military commander of his day, had not one but two grandiose baroque summer residences built by Johann Lukas von Hildebrandt on a low hill with exceptional views over the city center. The state rooms of the lower palace provide a fascinating insight into baroque interior design, and create an impressive backdrop for temporary exhibitions. ⏲ *45min. The quietest time to visit is during lunch-hour. Rennweg 6.* ☎ *01 795 5720-0. www.belvedere.at. €9.50 adults, €7.50 concessions, €3.50 kids (free under 5), €20 family (combined tickets with the Upper Belvedere are also available). Daily 10am–6pm (9pm on Wed). Tram 71 (Unteres Belvedere).*

⑦ ★★ kids Belvedere Gardens. The two Belvedere palaces are linked together by a strictly symmetrical French-style garden laid out on a gently sloping hill. Look out for the white marble fountains, stone sphinxes (symbols of strength and intelligence), and 12 charming *putti* (cherubic statues) on the steps (representing months of the year). On the upper terrace, the spectacular cityscape has barely changed over the centuries and is especially dramatic at sunset. Little wonder the palace is called 'Belvedere'

Statue from the Upper Belvedere— Prince Eugene's grand summer palace.

(Beautiful View). ⏲ *30min. Rennweg 6/Prinz-Eugen-Strasse 27.* ☎ *01 7984 1120. Apr–Oct 6am–6pm (until 8pm May–June, 9pm July–Aug), Nov–Mar 6.30am–6pm. Free. Tram 71 (Unteres Belvedere), Tram D (Schloss Belvedere).*

⑧ ★★★ Upper Belvedere. The finer of Prince Eugene's two summer palaces now contains the Austrian Gallery, with art dating from the Middle Ages to the present day. Medieval and baroque art is on the ground floor, with neoclassicism, Romanticism, and Viennese Biedermeier on the second floor. The real crowd-puller, however, is Austrian art from the 19th and 20th centuries, which includes the world's largest collection of works by Klimt.

⑨ ★★ Belvedere Café. This traditional café in the Upper Belvedere is the perfect spot to enjoy a drink and a gooey cream-cake after viewing the galleries. Try the specialty 'Klimt' coffee (served with amaretto cream)—it's delicious. *Prinz-Eugen-Strasse 27.* ☎ *01 798 8888. $–$$.*

⑩ ★★ Alpine & Botanical Gardens. Vienna's Botanical Gardens were created in the 18th-century to cultivate medicinal herbs. Few people discover the tiny adjoining Alpine Garden. It's one of my favorite spots to sit and relax in summer. ⏲ *45min. Landstrasser Gürtel 3.* ☎ *01 798 3149. www. bundesgarten.at. €3.20 adults, €2.80/€2.50 concessions, €1.30 kids (over 3). Daily 10am–6pm (last admission 5.30pm). Tram D (Schloss Belvedere).*

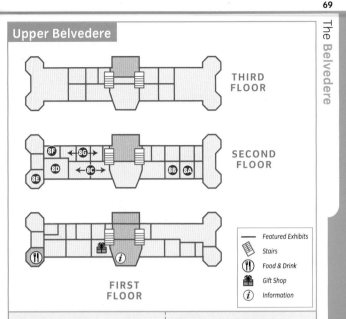

Upper Belvedere

THIRD FLOOR

SECOND FLOOR

FIRST FLOOR

— Featured Exhibits

Stairs

Food & Drink

Gift Shop

Information

Start on the first floor in the 'Vienna 1880–1900' section to admire an early Klimt portrait of **8A Sonja Knips (1898)** in an Impressionistic style, and **8B Spring at the Prater** by Tina Blau (1882). The next section—'Vienna around 1900'—marks a shift from historicism to modernity, through a series of **8C French Impressionist paintings** by Monet, Renoir, and Van Gogh. The highlights of the museum's Jugendstil collection are in Room 3, with Klimt's two famous 'golden phase' pictures: **8D The Kiss, and Judith**. Further noteworthy works by Klimt include **8E Adam and Eve (1917–18,**

Room 4) and the unfinished **8F Bride (1918, Room 5).** The remaining rooms move towards Expressionism with important works by **Schiele, Gerstl, Oppenheimer, Boeckl, and Munch**. ⏱ 1hr. Prinz-Eugen-Strasse 27. ☎ 01 795 57–0. www.belvedere.at. €9.50 adults, €7.50 concessions, €3.50 kids (free under 5), €20 family (combined tickets with the Lower Belvedere are also available), €3 audio guide, 30min guided tours cost €3 extra (11am, 12.30pm in German; 11.30am in English; noon in Italian). Daily 10am–6pm. Tram D (Schloss Belvedere).

11 ★★ kids Museum of Military History. Housed within the impressive, fortress-style Arsenal building, this superb museum presents the nation's military prowess from the 16th century to the present. ⏱ 1hr. Arsenal: Objekt 18,

Ghegastrasse. ☎ 01 795 61–0. www.hgm.or.at. €5.10 adults, €3.30 concessions, €7.30 family, free under 10, free on the first Sun of each month, €1.50 audio guide. Daily 9am–7pm, tank garden 9am–4.45pm. Tram D (Südbahnhof).

Schottenring & Alsergrund

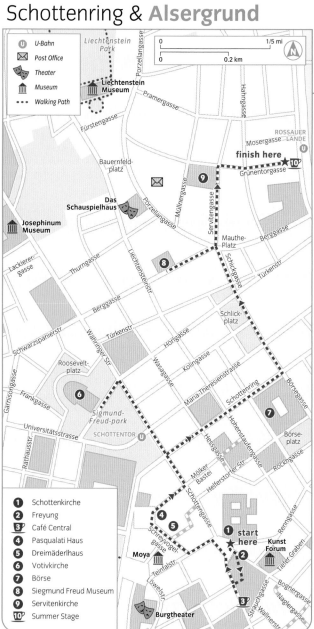

Legend:
- Ⓤ U-Bahn
- ✉ Post Office
- 🎭 Theater
- 🏛 Museum
- ••• Walking Path

0 — 1/5 mi
0 — 0.2 km

Liechtenstein Park
Liechtenstein Museum
Porzellangasse
Pramergasse
Hahngasse
Fürstengasse
Mosergasse
ROSSAUER LÄNDE
Bauernfeld-platz
finish here ★ 10'
Grünentorgasse
Das Schauspielhaus
Müllnergasse
Josephinum Museum
Servitengasse
Mauthe-Platz
Berggasse
Lackierer-gasse
Thurngasse
Liechtensteinstr.
Schickgasse
Türkenstr.
Berggasse
Türkenstr.
Hörlgasse
Schlick-platz
Schwarzspanierstr.
Währinger Str.
Waagasse
Kolingasse
Roosevelt-platz
Maria-Theresienstrasse
Schottenring
Börsegasse
Garnisongasse
Frankgasse
Sigmund-Freud-park
SCHOTTENTOR Ⓤ
Hohenstaufengasse
Börse-platz
Universitätsstrasse
Rockhgasse
Rathausstr.
Mölker Bastei
Helfersdorfer Str.
Hessgasse
Renngasse
Schottengasse
Schreyvogel-gasse
① start here ★
Kunst Forum
Moya
Teinfaltstr.
Dreimäder-haus
Löwelstr.
Burgtheater
Strauchgasse
Wallnerstr.
Bognergasse
Naglergasse
Tiefer Graben

1. Schottenkirche
2. Freyung
3. Café Central
4. Pasqualati Haus
5. Dreimäderlhaus
6. Votivkirche
7. Börse
8. Siegmund Freud Museum
9. Servitenkirche
10'. Summer Stage

These intimate districts just north of the city center claim a surprising variety of sights, from the Freyung's handsome palaces to the laid-back university district of Alsergrund. The Serviten quarter is especially picturesque: its cobbled streets, boutiques, and pavement cafés are Vienna's answer to Paris's St-Germain-des-Prés.

1 ★ Schottenkirche. Vienna's 'Scottish Church' has nothing to do with Scotland. It was founded in 1155 by Duke Heinrich II who brought monks to Vienna from Ireland (which was then known as Scotia Maior). The adjoining monastery (Schottenkloster) remained independent of ducal authority, and had the right to shelter asylum-seekers, hence the name of the square here—*Freyung* (from *frey* meaning 'free'). The church was remodeled during the baroque period, and it's worth a peep inside to see the rich if somewhat gloomy interior. Frustratingly, the main nave is locked to visitors except during services.
🕐 *10min. Freyung 6.* ☎ *01 5349 8200. www.schottenpfarre.at. Daily 9am–8pm. U-Bahn 2 (Schottentor).*

2 ★★★ Freyung. This spacious, triangular, cobbled square is essential viewing for architecture fans. Dominated by the Schottenkirche, it was once the city's main rubbish dump. Now, together with adjoining Herrengasse (Lord's Lane), it is lined with imposing baroque palaces formerly owned by the Viennese aristocracy. Many of these are currently used as government offices and embassies. They include the beautifully restored Palais Kinsky, Palais Harrach (where Joseph Haydn's

The Freyung's 'Austria Fountain'.

mother was the family cook), and Italianate-style Palais Ferstel, which housed the Vienna Stock Exchange until 1877. The quaint covered alleyways and courtyards of this district contain alluring boutiques and upmarket restaurants. Freyung Passage, leading to the famous Café Central (see below), is particularly elegant. In the middle of the square is the celebrated Austria Fountain, whose four bronze figures symbolize the principal rivers of Austria-Hungary (the Elbe, Vistula, Danube, and Po), crowned by an allegorical statue of Austria.

The Schottenkirche's tower dominates the Freyung square.

On alternate weekends the square is transformed into a farmers' market (☎ 0664 531 7301 for details), providing a chance to taste delicious organic produce from Lower Austria. *Freyung. U-Bahn 2 (Schottentor).*

3 ★★ **Café Central.** This splendid coffee house was once Vienna's most important literary rendezvous, frequented by eminent local writers such as Kraus, Bahr, and Altenberg. Trotsky used to play chess with Stalin under the vaulted arches. Now popular with tourists, it serves reliable (if pricey) café cuisine. *Herrengasse 14 (corner Strauchgasse).* ☎ 01 533 3764–26. $$.

4 ★★★ **Pasqualati Haus.** *See p 37, bullet* **1**.

5 ★ **Dreimäderlhaus.** Just round the corner from the Pasqualati Haus, you'll find one of Vienna's most appealing Biedermeier houses. Legend has it three sweethearts (*drei Mäderl*) of Franz Schubert once lived here, as recounted in the 1920s' operetta of the same name, which contains the Viennese composer's

Votivkirche—easy to confuse in appearance with Stephansdom.

Café Central—a celebrated tourist honey-pot.

melodies. *Schreyvogelgasse 10. U-Bahn 2 (Schottentor).*

6 ★ **Votivkirche.** The striking white sandstone Votive Church, designed by Heinrich von Ferstel, was erected as a thanksgiving after a failed attempt on the life of Emperor Franz Joseph in 1853. It was one of the first buildings constructed on the new Ringstrasse, and is Vienna's most important example of the neo-Gothic style, distinguished by its patterned roof and lacy twin spires. The interior is rather impersonal, but it does contain some notable frescoes and a carved altar depicting the Passion of Christ. *Rooseveltplatz 8.* ☎ 01 405 1192. www.votivkirche.at. *Sun 9am–1pm, Tues–Sat 9am–1pm, 4pm–6pm, closed Mon. U-Bahn 2 (Schottentor).*

7 ★ **Börse.** Vienna's Stock Exchange is one of the most elegant buildings on the Ringstrasse. Constructed in 1877 by the acclaimed architect Theophil Hansen (who also built the Parlament and Burgtheater), it is noteworthy for its handsome red brickwork (known locally as *Hansenrot*) and white stonework cornices. *Schottenring 20.* ☎ 01 531 650.

Closed to visitors. U-Bahn 2 (Schottentor).

8 ★ **Siegmund Freud Museum.** One of Vienna's most famous citizens, the physician Siegmund Freud (1856–1939) lived in this apartment for most of his life. The museum has few original artifacts or furnishings, but a fascinating photo-gallery casts a revealing light on the father of psychoanalysis. For decades, Freud was regarded as a leading figure in world of medicine, but his Jewish background prevented him from becoming a professor of Vienna's University until 1902. He was eventually driven from the city by the Nazis in 1937. ⏲ *30min. Burggasse 19.* ☎ *01 319 1596. www.freud-museum.at. €7 adults, €5.50/€4.50 concessions, €2.50 kids. €2 audio guide. Daily 9am–5pm (6pm July–Sept). U-Bahn 2 (Schottentor).*

9 ★ **Servitenkirche.** You'll find this little church in the middle of the atmospheric Serviten quarter. Even though it is a little out of the way, it's worth a visit to admire the extravagant baroque interior, which served as a model for the Karlskirche. Frustratingly, you have to peer through iron railings, as the nave is only open during services. *Servitengasse 9.* ☎ *01 317 6195–0. U-Bahn 4 (Rossauer Lände).*

10 ★★★ **kids Summer Stage.** A holiday atmosphere spreads along the Danube Canal during the summer months. This lively open-air bar and restaurant zone, open from May through September, offers plenty for all the family. Tempting eateries and cool cocktail bars line the canal banks, providing live music and entertainment most nights. Try **Oasia** (☎ 0699 8128 5540, $) for Asian cuisine or **Piranha** (☎ 0699 1501 5013, $–$$) for steaks and burgers. There's also trampolining, boules, beach volleyball, and a kids' club at weekends. *Rossauer Lände.* ☎ *01 315 5202. Mon–Sat 5pm–1am, Sun 3pm–1am. U-Bahn 4 (Rossauer Lände).*

Dine al fresco at the Summer Stage.

The MuseumsQuartier (MQ)

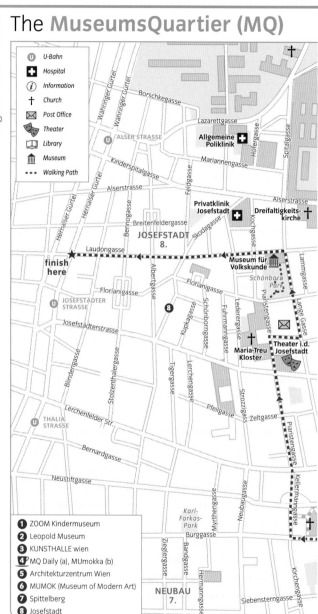

Legend:
- Ⓤ U-Bahn
- ✚ Hospital
- ⓘ Information
- † Church
- ✉ Post Office
- 🎭 Theater
- 📖 Library
- 🏛 Museum
- ••• Walking Path

1. ZOOM Kindermuseum
2. Leopold Museum
3. KUNSTHALLE wien
4. MQ Daily (a), MUmokka (b)
5. Architekturzentrum Wien
6. MUMOK (Museum of Modern Art)
7. Spittelberg
8. Josefstadt

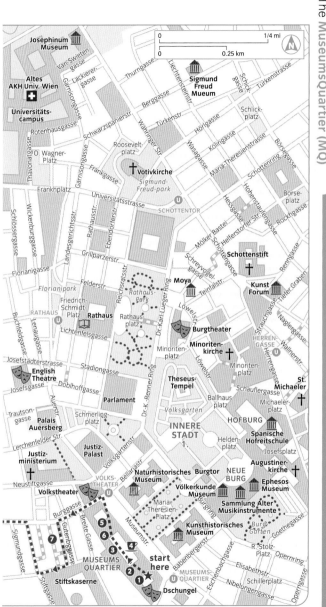

It would be easy to spend all day at the MuseumsQuartier (Museum Quarter)—one of Vienna's most popular areas. It has a superb mix of modern architecture, world-class galleries, and family attractions. However, just round the corner, two of the city's most attractive and beguiling quarters also await your discovery—Spittelberg and Josefstadt—with their cobbled streets and enticing bars and restaurants.

Relax in the MQ complex.

❶ ★★★ kids ZOOM Kindermuseum. A superb interactive museum devoted solely to kids. See p 44, bullet ❼.

❷ ★★★ Leopold Museum. This major gallery hosts a leading collection of 19th- and 20th-century Austrian art, belonging to Viennese *aficionados* Rudolf and Elizabeth Leopold. The main Jugendstil and Secessionist collections are on the ground floor, alongside some important canvases by Klimt, Gerstl, and Moser, but the main draw is the world's largest assembly of works by Egon Schiele.

❸ ★ KUNSTHALLE wien. The temporary exhibitions of modern art at the Vienna Art Gallery enjoy international repute, despite their location within an architecturally unremarkable red-brick building. *Museumsplatz 1. ☎ 01 521 8933. www.kunsthallewien.at. €7.50 adults €6/€4 concessions (depending on exhibition). Daily 10am–7pm (until 10pm Thurs). U-Bahn 2 (Museumsquartier).*

❹ ★★ kids My two favorite lunch spots here are the cheap, family-friendly **MQ Daily** (Museumsplatz 1, ☎ 01 522 4524, $) for soups, salads, and pasta; or the more sophisticated **MUmokka** terrace café (Museumsplatz 1, ☎ 01 525 001 440, $$), which serves tempting open sandwiches, cheese platters, and fresh juices.

❺ ★ Architekturzentrum Wien. This small Architecture Center provides a vivid account of 20th- and 21st-century Austrian architecture, through models, interactive displays, and photographs. The only controversial omission is Hundertwasser (see p 22), who is apparently considered to be more of an artist than an architect. ⏱ *45min. Museumsplatz 1. ☎ 01 522 3115. www.azw.at. Daily 10am–7pm. €5 adults, €3.50 concessions, €8 family, free under 6. U-Bahn 2/3 (Volkstheater).*

❻ ★ MUMOK (Museum of Modern Art). The dramatic cuboid exterior of the Museum of Modern Art (MOMUK) is undeniably impressive, clad in sleek gray basalt. The interior, although it lacks natural

Leopold Museum

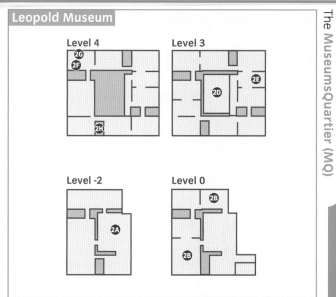

Level 4

Level 3

Level -2

Level 0

The lower ground floor contains the great **2A Egon Schiele Collection** with numerous drawings by one of the most notable early Existentialists and Expressionists, including the poignant *Mother and Daughter* (1913) and *Edith Schiele in a Striped Dress* (1915). On the ground floor, the **2B Jugendstil and Secessionist paintings** include canvases by Schiele, Gerstl, and Klimt. The **2C second-floor café** is worth a stop, before moving on to the brilliant collection of **2D Expressionist and inter-war paintings** on the 3rd floor. The real gems here are works by Schiele (including *Self-Portrait* —1910), Kokoschka, Huber, Boeckl, and

Oppenheimer; and the **2E winter landscapes of Alfons Walde**, who worked for years to perfect his portrayal of snow. The 4th floor contains yet more impressive paintings by Klimt, including **Attersee** (1901), and the celebrated **2F Death and Life** (1911–15). Some exquisite **2G Wiener Werkstätte furniture** and decorative items by Moser, Loos, and Hoffmann can also be seen on this floor. ◷ *2hr. Museumsplatz.* ☎ *01 525 70–0. www.leopoldmuseum.org. €10 adults, €6.50 concessions, €3 audio guide. Daily 10am–7pm (until 10pm Thurs). U-Bahn 2 (Museumsquartier).*

light, contains a significant collection of modern and contemporary art, covering a broad spectrum of genres from Cubism and Expressionism to Photo Realism, Fluxus, and Nouveau Réalisme. Its

acclaimed Pop Art section contains works by Warhol, Jasper Johns, Liechtenstein, and Rauschenberg. The highly controversial Viennese Actionism collection—one of the most extreme of all modern-art

The distinctive grey basalt façade of the Museum of Modern Art (MUMOK).

movements—is the largest in the world. Frustratingly, only a small selection of the museum's artworks is ever on view at a time. ⏱ *1hr. Museumsplatz 1. ☎ 01 52500. www.mumok.at. €9 adults, €6.50 concessions, €7.20 OAPs. Daily 10am–6pm (to 9pm Thurs) U-Bahn 2/3 (Volkstheater).*

7 ★★★ **Spittelberg.** Just behind the MuseumsQuartier (between Breitergasse, Siebensterngasse, Sigmundgasse, and Burggasse), this romantic, pedestrianized district of narrow, cobbled streets—with pretty Biedermeier houses and fountain-splashed squares—epitomizes old-world Vienna at its most appealing. Formerly a red-light district servicing the nearby barracks, Spittelberg became a fashionable place to live in the 1970s and is now one of the city's most desirable addresses: an enclave of galleries, cosy *Beisls* (traditional Austrian country-style inns), and pavement cafés. The Christmas market held here is one of Vienna's best (and certainly the most picturesque), selling high-quality handicrafts and *Glühwein. www.spittelberg.at. U-Bahn 2/3 (Volkstheater).*

8 ★★ **Josefstadt.** When I've had my fill of the grand museums and monumental architecture in the city center, one of my favorite districts to explore is Josefstadt, named after Josef I, as the plans for the area were laid out during his reign. This genteel residential quarter still feels like an 18th-century Viennese village, with its mix of Biedermeier architecture, handsome churches, curious shops, and small leafy parks. At its heart is the popular Josefstadt Theater (Vienna's oldest), and some friendly bars and restaurants. The Maria Treu Kirche (1716) is the finest church here, containing an organ once played by the composer Anton Bruckner. Bring your binoculars to examine the frescoes on its splendid baroque ceiling. Beethoven's funeral took place in the nearby Dreifaltigkeitskirche (Holy Trinity Church) in 1827. Just round the corner, the charming Museum für Völkskunde (Folklore Museum) portrays rural Austrian life through handcrafted sculptures, rural paintings, and furniture from throughout the region. Josefstadt's elegance fades as you approach the Gürtel ring-road, where a host of late-night bars and clubs compete for your attention. *Josefstadt. Volkskundemuseum: Laudongasse 15–18. ☎ 01 406 8905. www.volkskundemuseum.at. €5 adults, €3.50 kids, €9 family. Tues–Sun 10am–5pm. Tram 5/33 or Bus 13A (Laudongasse).* ●

Atnon Bruckner once played at the Maria Treu Kirche in Josefstadt.

The Best Shopping

Shopping Best Bets

Most **Trendy Interior Design**
★★ das möbel > das geschäft, *Gumpendorferstraße 11 (p 85)*

Best for **Gourmands**
★★★ Meinl am Graben, *Graben 19 (p 88)*

Best **Austrian Designs**
★★★ artup, *Bauernmarkt 8 (p 87)*

Best **Boutique for Fashionistas**
★★ Mühlbauer Mode, *Seilergasse 5 (p 87)*

Best **Foot Forward**
★★★ Ludwig Reiter, *Mölkersteig 1 (p 87)*

Best **Hot-Date Lingerie**
★★ Wolford, *Graben 16 (p 88)*

Best for **Chocoholics**
★★★ Xocolat, *Freyung 2 (Im Passage) (p 90)*

Best **Quirky Gifts**
★★★ MAK Design Shop, *Stubenring 5 (p 92)*

Best **Picnic Supplies**
★★★ Naschmarkt, *Naschmarkt (p 89)*

Most **Unusual Shop**
★★★ phil, *Gumpendorferstrasse 10-12 (p 86)*

Most **Environmentally Friendly Lifestyle**
★ Grüne Erde, *Mariahilferstrasse 9 (p 86)*

Best for **Posh Porcelain**
★★★ Augarten, *Stock-im-Eisen-Platz 3 (p 85)*

Best for **Maps & Travel Guides**
★★ Freytag & Berndt, *Kohlmarkt 9 (p 85)*

Most **Stylish Jugendstil Souvenirs**
★★ Lichterloh, *Gumpendorferstrasse 15-17 (p 86)*

Best for **Treasure-Hunting**
★★ Dorotheum, *Dorotheergasse 17 (p 85)*

Best for **Classical Music**
★★ Arcadia, *Kärtnerstrasse 40 (p 92)*

Best **Lederhosen**
★★★ Tostmann Trachten, *Schottengasse 3a (p 88)*

Best **Glass**
★★ J & L Lobmeyr, *Kärtnerstrasse 26 (p 86)*; ★★ Swarovski, *Kärtnerstrasse 8 (p 91)*

Best **Cakes**
★★★ Sacher Confiserie, *Philharmonikerstrasse 4 (p 89)*; ★★★ Demel, *Kohlmarkt 14 (p 88)*

Best to **Placate the Kids**
★★★ Mädchen und Buben, *Servitengasse 4A (p 90)*

Mozart gets everywhere. Here he is selling chocolates!

Shopping Around Kärtnerstrasse

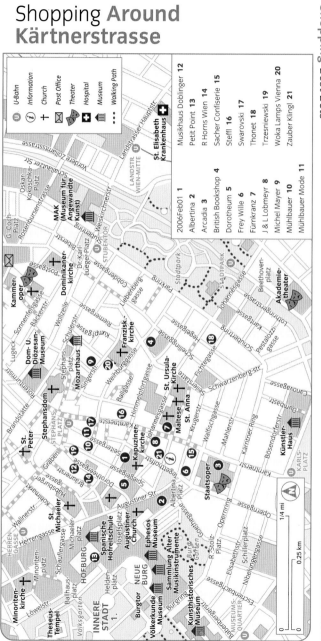

Key

- 🚇 U-Bahn
- ⓘ Information
- ✝ Church
- 🖃 Post Office
- 🎭 Theater
- ✚ Hospital
- 🏛 Museum
- ⋯ Walking Path

2006Feb01 **1**
Albertina **2**
Arcadia **3**
British Bookshop **4**
Dorotheum **5**
Frey Wille **6**
Fürnkranz **7**
J & L Lobmeyr **8**
Michel Mayer **9**
Mühlbauer **10**
Mühlbauer Mode **11**

Musikhaus Doblinger **12**
Petit Point **13**
R Horns Wien **14**
Sacher Confiserie **15**
Steffl **16**
Swarovski **17**
Thonet **18**
Trzesniewski **19**
Woka Lamps Vienna **20**
Zauber Klingl **21**

Shopping **City Center North**

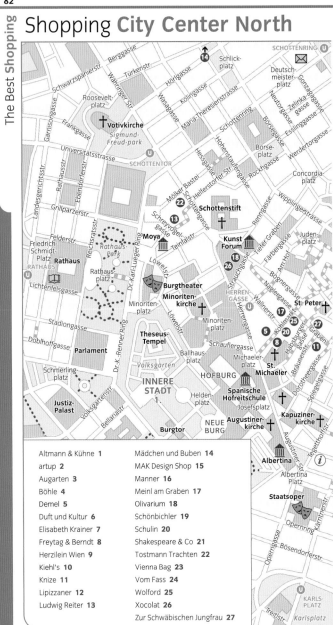

Altmann & Kühne **1**

artup **2**

Augarten **3**

Böhle **4**

Demel **5**

Duft und Kultur **6**

Elisabeth Krainer **7**

Freytag & Berndt **8**

Herzilein Wien **9**

Kiehl's **10**

Knize **11**

Lipizzaner **12**

Ludwig Reiter **13**

Mädchen und Buben **14**

MAK Design Shop **15**

Manner **16**

Meinl am Graben **17**

Olivarium **18**

Schönbichler **19**

Schulin **20**

Shakespeare & Co **21**

Tostmann Trachten **22**

Vienna Bag **23**

Vom Fass **24**

Wolford **25**

Xocolat **26**

Zur Schwäbischen Jungfrau **27**

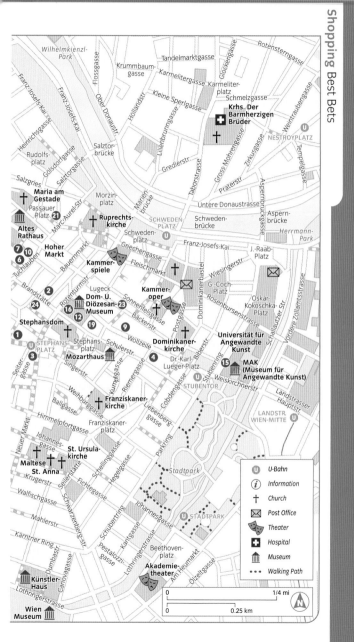

Shopping **Mariahilf & Neubau**

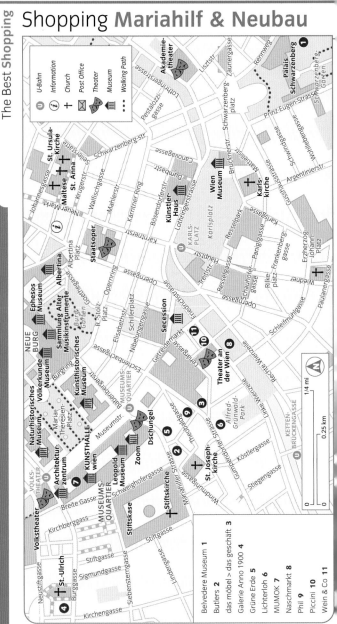

U-Bahn
i Information
+ Church
⊠ Post Office
▥ Theater
▥ Museum
⋯ Walking Path

Akademie-theater
Palais Schwarzenberg ❶
Rennweg
Liszstr.
Zäunergasse
Prinz-Eugen-Strasse
Schwarzenberg-platz
Schwarzenberg-str.
Pestalozzi-gasse
St. Ursula-Kirche
St. Anna
St. Maltese
Neuer Markt
Johannesgasse
Schwarzenberg-str.
Seilerstätte
Krugerstr.
Wallischgasse
Mahlerstr.
Kärntner Ring
Canovagasse
Dumbastr.
Bösendorferstrasse
Künstler-Haus
Wien Museum ▥
Karls-kirche
Argentinierstr.
Matteistr.
Brucknerstr.
Lothringerstrasse
Karlsplatz
Resselpark
Karlsgasse
Staatsoper ▥
Kärntnerstr.
i
Lothringerstr.
KARLS PLATZ
Hauptstr.
Erzherzog Johann Platz
Albertina
Albertina Platz
Opernring
Operngasse
Treitlstr.
Resselgasse
Schaufler-gasse
Panigl-gasse
Frankenberg-gasse
Rilke-platz
Ephesos Museum ▥
Sammlung Alter Musikinstrumente ▥
Burg Garten
R. Stolz-Platz
Elisabethstr.
Schillerplatz
Secession ▥
Friedrichstrasse
Nibelungengasse
Getreidemarkt
❶❶
❶⓪
Theater an der Wien
Schleifmühlgasse
Margareten-str.
NEUE BURG
Kunsthistorisches Museum ▥
Burgring
Babenbergerstr.
MUSEUMS-QUARTIER
Eschenbachgasse
Lehargasse
❽
Rechte Wienzeile
Naturhistorisches Museum ▥
Völkerkunde Museum ▥
Architektur-zentrum ▥
KUNSTHALLE wien ▥
Maria-Theresien-Platz
Museumstr.
Dschungel
❼
❺
❷
❾
❸
Theobaldgasse
Alfred-Grünwald-Park
Linke Wienzeile
VOLKS-THEATER
MUSEUMS-QUARTIER
Leopold Museum ▥
Zoom ▥
Schweighofergasse
Mariahilfer Strasse
Windmühlgasse
St. Joseph-kirche
Gumpendorfer Strasse
Köstlergasse
Volkstheater ▥
Breite Gasse
Stiftskirche +
Kirchberggass
Stiftskase
Stiftgasse
Siebensterngass
Mariahilfer Strasse
Stiftgasse
St. Joseph-kirche +
Stiegengasse
KETTEN-BRÜCKENGASSE
St. Ulrich + ❹
Neustiftgasse
Burggasse
Stiftgasse
Sigmundsgasse
Lindengasse
Kirchengasse

N ⊿

0   1/4 mi
0   0.25 km

Belvedere Museum **1**
Butlers **2**
das möbel > das geschäft **3**
Galerie Anno 1900 **4**
Grüne Erde **5**
Lichterloh **6**
MUMOK **7**
Naschmarkt **8**
Phil **9**
Piccini **10**
Wein & Co **11**

Vienna **Shopping A to Z**

Art & Antiques

★★ Dorotheum CITY CENTER
Pick up some unusual and authentic treasures at this world-renowned auction house, which holds regular sales of paintings, furniture, jewelry, decorative objects, and toys. *Dorotheergasse 17.* ☎ *01 515 60-0. www.dorotheum.at. AE, DC, MC, V. U-Bahn 1/3 (Stephansplatz). Map p 81.*

★ Galerie Anno 1900 NEUBAU
Quaint and quirky, this Aladdin's Cave is full of specialist Art Deco and Jugendstil antiques—especially ornaments, glassware, clocks, and lamps. *Burggasse 24 (corner Kirchengasse).* ☎ *01 523 8477. AE, DC, MC, V. U-Bahn 2/3 (Volkstheater). Map p 84.*

Beauty Products

★★ Kiehl's CITY CENTER   It's hard to believe this cult cosmetics brand started out over 150 years ago in a small New York apothecary. This is Austria's only branch. Their 'Facial Fuel' moisturizer is a great pick-me-up for weary travelers. *Tuchlauben 23.* ☎ *01 532 2011. www.kiehls.com. AE, DC, MC, V. U-Bahn 3 (Herrengasse). Map p 82.*

★ Olivarium SCHOTTENRING
Pamper yourself with delicious soaps, toiletries, and beauty products—all made with olive oil. Also olives, oils, *tapenades*, and hand-carved olivewood items. *Passage im Palais Ferstel, Freyung 2.* ☎ *01 252 3535. www.olivarium.com. DC, MC, V. U-Bahn 3 (Herrengasse). Map p 82.*

Books & Maps

★ British Bookshop CITY CENTER   There's an excellent choice of English-language volumes here, from the latest blockbuster novels and kids' books to coffee-table books about Vienna. *Weihburggasse 24.* ☎ *01 512 1945. www.britishbookshop.at. AE, DC, MC, V. U-Bahn 3 (Stubentor). Map p 81.*

★★ Freytag & Berndt CITY CENTER   A staggering collection of maps and travel guides (many in English) on Vienna, the Wienerwald, Austria, and the rest of the world, housed in a magnificent Jugendstil house. *Kohlmarkt 9.* ☎ *01 533 8685. www.freytagberndt.at. AE, DC, MC, V. U-Bahn 3 (Herrengasse). Map p 82.*

★★ Shakespeare & Co CITY CENTER   I could spend hours browsing in this higgledy-piggledy, old-fashioned bookshop, containing a huge array of English-language books (including Austrian authors in translation). *Sterngasse 2.* ☎ *01 535 5053. www.shakespeare.co.at. MC. V. U-Bahn 1/4 (Schwedenplatz). Map p 82.*

Design & Interiors

★★★ Augarten CITY CENTER
Some of the exquisite patterns of the former imperial porcelain manufacturer are centuries old, including hand-decorated rose chinaware, designed in the 18th century for Empress Maria Theresa. *Stock-im-Eisen-Platz 3.* ☎ *01 512 1494. www.augarten.at. AE, DC, MC, V. U-Bahn 1/3 (Stephansplatz). Map p 82.*

★ Butlers NEUBAU   This jam-packed shop is full of tempting ideas for holiday gifts, including fun household gadgets and interesting knick-knacks. *Mariahilferstrasse 17.* ☎ *01 585 7108. www.butlers.at. MC, V. U-Bahn 2 (Museumsquartier). Map p 84.*

★★ das möbel > das geschäft MQ   This spacious store, laid out like an exclusive apartment, is *the* place for seriously cool furniture and innovative accessories by young up-and-coming Austrian designers. *Gumpendorfer Straße 11.* ☎ *01 924 3834. www.dasmoebel.at. MC, V. U-Bahn 2 (Museumsquartier). Map p 84.*

★ **Grüne Erde** MQ A modish lifestyle department store, containing stylish, eco-friendly household items, kitchen utensils, ceramics, candles, and other home comforts. *Mariahilferstrasse 9.* ☎ *07615 203 410. www.grueneerde.at. AE, DC, MC, V. U-Bahn 2 (Museumsquartier). Map p 84.*

★★ **Lichterloh** MQ This ultra-hip shop is filled with iconic designer furniture, *objets d'art* ,and lighting from Art Deco through pop art to classic modernism. *Gumpendorfer-strasse 15-17.* ☎ *01 586 0520. www. lichterloh.com. AE, DC, MC, V. U-Bahn 2 (Museumsquartier). Map p 84.*

★★ **J & L Lobmeyr** CITY CENTER The former imperial glass-makers specialize in fine crystal glassware—rejuvenating designs from the Wiener Werkstätte in their glamorous chandelier-lit showroom. *Kärtner-strasse 26.* ☎ *01 512 0508. www. lobmeyr.at. AE, DC, MC, V. U-Bahn 1/3 (Stephansplatz). Map p 81.*

★★★ **phil** MQ No two chairs or tables are alike in this unusual café/shop, where guests come not just to eat and drink but also to buy the constantly changing retro furniture. *Gumpendorferstrasse 10-12.* ☎ *01 581 0489. www.phil.info. MC, V. U-Bahn 2 (Museumsquartier). Map p 84.*

★ **Thonet** CITY CENTER This flagship store is famous for inventing bentwood chairs in the early 19th century. They are still sold today alongside other fashionable items of furniture. ☎ *01 310 2002-0. www.thonet-vienna.com. MC, V. Tram 1/2/D (Schwarzenberg-platz). Map p 81.*

★ **Woka Lamps Vienna** CITY CENTER Specialists in early 20th-century light designs, with authentic handmade replicas of Bauhaus, Jugendstil, and Secessionist lamps (plus some originals too). *Singer-strasse 16.* ☎ *01 513 2912. www. woka.com. AE, DC, MC, V. U-Bahn 1/3 (Stephansplatz). Map p 81.*

★ **Zur Schwäbischen Jungfrau** CITY CENTER Buy upmarket, luxurious table- and bed-linen, eider-down quilts, and swimwear in this grand, old-fashioned shop with

Phil's—Not just a shop, but a café too.

stucco ceilings and chandeliers. *Graben 26.* ☎ *01 535 5356. www. schwaebischen-jungfrau.at. AE, DC, MC, V. U-Bahn 1/3 (Stephansplatz). Map p 82.*

Fashion & Accessories

★★ **2006Feb01** CITY CENTER Top designer fashions for men and women, in an architecturally striking, very fashionable shop near Stephansdom, offering exemplary service. *Plankengasse 3.* ☎ *01 513 4222. www.2006feb01.com. AE, DC, MC, V. U-Bahn 1/3 (Stephansplatz). Map p 81.*

★★★ **artup** CITY CENTER My favorite shop for Austrian style—with bright, stylish, often unusual, and at times eccentric fashion, jewelry, ceramics, and accessories by new designers. *Bauernmarkt 8.* ☎ *01 535 5097. www.artup.at. DC, MC, V. U-Bahn 1/3 (Stephansplatz). Map p 82.*

★★ **Fürnkranz Couture** CITY CENTER Get your ball gowns at one of Vienna's most exclusive fashion boutiques. The top address for evening wear, including luxurious creations by couturiers such as Armani, Lacroix, and Valentino. *Kärntner strasse 39.* ☎ *01 488 4426. www.fuernkranz.com. AE, DC, MC, V. U-Bahn 1/3 (Stephansplatz). Map p 81.*

★★ **Knize** CITY CENTER This old-fashioned, wood-paneled shop, created by interior-design genius Adolf Loos, offers classy, tailor-made and *prêt-à-porter* menswear, with traditional service at its finest. *Graben 13.* ☎ *01 512 2119. www.knize.at. AE, DC, MC, V. U-Bahn 1/3 (Stephansplatz). Map p 82.*

★★★ **Ludwig Reiter** SCHOTTEN-RING Arnold Schwarzenegger buys his shoes at this elegant family establishment in a beautiful Biedermeier house. It sells ladies' footwear too. *Mölkersteig 1.* ☎ *01 533 420 422. www.ludwig-reiter.com. AE, DC, MC, V. U-Bahn 2 (Schottentor). Map p 82.*

★★★ **Michel Mayer** CITY CENTER Mix and match daytime separates and rub shoulders with floaty feminine designs in extravagant fabrics at this *bijou* designer boutique. *Singerstrasse 7.* ☎ *01 967 4055. www. michelmayer.at. AE, MC, V. U-Bahn 1/3 (Stephansplatz). Map p 81.*

★★ **Mühlbauer** CITY CENTER Eye-catching modern millinery and accessories add the finishing touches to any outfit at this spacious, sophisticated shop. *Seilergasse 10.* ☎ *01 512 2241. www. muehlbauer.at. AE, DC, MC, V. U-Bahn 1/3 (Stephansplatz). Map p 81.*

★★ **Mühlbauer Mode** CITY CENTER The labels at this shop should set any keen fashionista's pulse racing. In a modern setting of black-and-white minimalism, it stocks state-of-the-art creations by local and international designers. *Seilergasse 5.* ☎ *01 513 7070. AE, DC,MC, V. www.muehlbauer.at. U-Bahn 1/3 (Stephansplatz). Map p 81.*

★★★ **R Horns Wien** CITY CENTER Visit this internationally celebrated designer to buy stylish but functional leatherware: purses, bags, briefcases—perhaps some extra luggage to carry all your souvenirs home. *Bräunerstrasse 7.* ☎ *01 513 8294. www.rhorns.com. AE, DC, MC, V. U-Bahn 3 (Herrengasse). Map p 81.*

★★★ **Steffl** CITY CENTER Vienna's top department store sells high-end fashions, trendy mainstream collections, and chic lifestyle artifacts to brand-conscious customers. *Kärntnerstrasse 19.* ☎ *01 514 31-0. www.kaufhaus-steffl.at. AE, DC, MC, V. U-Bahn 1/3 (Stephansplatz). Map p 81.*

★★★ Tostmann Trachten

SCHOTTENRING   For traditional Austrian fashions and hand-embroidered *dirndls, lederhosen,* felt slippers, and beautiful patchwork in a genial rustic setting. *Schottengasse 3a.* ☎ *01 533 5331. www.tostmann. at. AE, DC, MC, V. U-Bahn 2 (Schottentor). Map p 82.*

★★ Vienna Bag CITY CENTER

A tiny shop displaying feather-light, ultra-chic handbags of deceptive simplicity made of fibreglass. They come in a dazzling range of colors, including my favorites—apple green and fuchsia, and are currently all the rage. *Bäckerstrasse 7.* ☎ *01 513 1184. www.vienna-bag.at. DC, MC, V. U-Bahn 1/3 (Stephansplatz). Map p 82.*

★★ Wolford CITY CENTER   Aus-

tria's best-known fashion brand is famed for its high-quality hosiery, but Wolford has now diversified into slinky lingerie and flattering swimwear. *Graben 16.* ☎ *01 535 1576. www.wolford.com. AE, DC, MC, V. U-Bahn 1/3 (Stephansplatz). Map p 82.*

Food & Wines

★★ Altmann & Kühne CITY CEN-

TER   The trademark mini-chocolates sold by this old-fashioned confectioner make perfect gifts, beautifully packaged in tiny handmade boxes decorated with traditional Viennese scenes. *Graben 30.* ☎ *01 533 0927. www.altmann-kuehne.at. AE, DC, MC, V. U-Bahn 1/3 (Stephansplatz). Map p 82.*

★★★ Böhle CITY CENTER   This

miniscule deli-bistro is gourmand heaven, crammed with delectable treats: fine cheeses, charcuterie, preserves and pickles, cakes, superior wines, and seasonal fruit and vegetables. *Wollzeile 30.* ☎ *01 512 3155. www.boehle.at. DC, MC, V. U-Bahn 3 (Stubentor). Map p 82.*

There's always a mouth-watering display at the former Imperial confectionery, Demel.

★★★ Demel CITY CENTER   The

imperial confectioners have baked cakes and sweets for the rich and famous for several centuries, and the proof is in the eating. These traditional tearooms are pricey but popular. *Kohlmarkt 14.* ☎ *01 535 1717-0. www.demel.at. AE, DC, MC, V. U-Bahn 3 (Herrengasse). Map p 82.*

★★★ Meinl am Graben CITY

CENTER   Vienna's top delicatessen is known for its superb coffee, tea, chocolates, wines, and its impressive array of top-notch produce from Austria and around the world. *Graben 19.* ☎ *01 532 3334. www.meinlamgraben.at. AE, DC, MC, V. U-Bahn 3 (Herrengasse). Map p 82.*

★★★ Lipizzaner CITY CENTER

Delicious Lipizzaner chocolates (a white-chocolate version of the ubiquitous *Mozartkugel* (Mozart chocolates), *Lipizzanertorten,* and other horse-themed treats are the specialties here. *Stephansplatz 6.* ☎ *01 512 5455. www.lipizzaner-austria. com. AE, DC, MC, V. U-Bahn 1/3 (Stephansplatz). Map p 82.*

★★ Manner CITY CENTER
Vienna's favorite biscuit—a delicious blend of wafer and hazelnut cream—makes an ideal snack to keep you going between museums and galleries. *Stephansplatz 7.* ☎ *01 513 7018. www.manner.com. AE, DC, MC, V. U-Bahn 1/3 (Stephans-platz). Map p 82.*

★★★ Naschmarkt NASCHMARKT
Vienna's best and liveliest produce market is the perfect place to shop for a picnic, but with such a bewildering choice of food-stalls it's difficult to know where to start. Appealing stands to look out for include Strmiska (248) for superb *sauerkraut* and pickled gherkins; Käseland (172) or Der Urbanek (46) for cheese and cold cuts; Poehl (158) for breads and olive oil; Gegenbauer (111–114) for unusual, flavored vinegars; and Oberlaa (175) for cakes and confectionery. *Naschmarkt. Stalls: Mon–Fri 8am–6pm, Sat 6am–1pm. U-Bahn 1/2/4 Karlsplatz, U4 Kettenbrückengasse.*

Meinl - the best coffee in town.

Käseland—a paradise for cheese lovers at the Naschmarkt.

★★ Piccini NASCHMARKT Not only does this Italian delicatessen sell sensational *antipasti*, cold cuts, cheese, olives, oils, *biscotti*, nougat, and wine, but it also has an adjoining gourmet restaurant. *Linke Wienzeile 4.* ☎ *01 587 5254. MC, V. U-Bahn 1/2/4 (Karlsplatz). Map p 84.*

★★★ Sacher Confiserie CITY CENTER Indulge yourself with Vienna's most celebrated cake—the rich, chocolate *Sachertorte*. You can even ship them home beautifully packaged in wooden boxes of varying sizes. *Philharmonikerstrasse 4.* ☎ *01 514 56–0. www.sacher.com. AE, DC, MC, V. Tram D/J/1/2 (Oper). Map p 81.*

★★ Schönbichler CITY CENTER
A fragrant, wood-paneled shop, selling over 150 varieties of teas, teapots, storage jars, and other tea accessories. Seasonal blends include 'snowflake tea' and 'Christmas tea'. *Wollzeile 4. www.schoenbichler.at.* ☎ *01 512 1816. AE, DC, MC, V. U-Bahn (Stephansplatz). Map p 82.*

★ Trześniewski CITY CENTER
This tiny, old-fashioned bar/shop sells the most delicious, bite-sized

Vienna's traditional wooden toys always make special presents.

open sandwiches, just right for preventing hunger pangs during shopping or sightseeing. *Dorotheergasse 1.* ☎ *01 512 3291. www.speckmitei. at. No credit cards. U-Bahn 1/3 (Stephansplatz). Map p 81.*

★★ **Vom Fass** CITY CENTER Choose your container from an attractive display, then decide what to put in it from an enormous selection of oils, vinegars, schnapps, liqueurs, and whiskies. *Brandstätte 5.* ☎ *01 532 2525. www.vomfass-wiencity.at. MC, V. U-Bahn 1/3 (Stephansplatz). Map p 82.*

★★ **Wein & Co** NASCHMARKT This specialist wine supermarket offers a comprehensive selection of wines from around the globe, including some excellent Austrian wines at affordable prices. Try before you buy in the adjoining winebar! *Getreidemarkt 1.* ☎ *01 585 7257. www.weinco.at. AE, DC, MC, V. U-Bahn 1/2/4 (Karlsplatz). Map p 84.*

★★★ **Xocolat** SCHOTTENRING Essential viewing for chocoholics, this little shop displays an eye-popping selection of bar chocolate,

flavored cocoa powders, sauces, and fondue mixtures. *Freyung 2 (Im Passage).* ☎ *01 535 4363. www.xocolat. at. AE, DC, MC, V. U-Bahn 3 (Herrengasse). Map p 82.*

For Kids

★★★ **Herzilein Wien** CITY CENTER A pretty pastel-colored shop containing adorable clothing for boys and girls (under nine), shoes, tasteful toys and teddies, and gorgeous appliquéd bed-linen. *Wollzeile 17.* ☎ *0699 1092 9654. www. herzilein-wien.at. AE, DC, MC, V. U-Bahn 3 (Stubentor). Map p 82.*

★★★ **Mädchen und Buben** SCHOTTENRING This small, neighborhood toyshop is great for gift-hunting, brimful of appealing dolls, puppets, educational games, and old-fashioned wooden toys. *Servitengasse 4A.* ☎ *01 968 6233. www.handpuppen.at. AE, DC, MC, V. U-Bahn 4 (Rossauer Lände). Map p 82.*

★★ **Zauber Klingl** CITY CENTER An enchanting choice of fancy-dress costumes, party decorations, magicians' tricks, accessories, and gimmicks is on display at this long-established emporium. *Fuhrich-strasse 6.* ☎ *01 512 6868. MC, V. Tram D/J/1/2 (Oper). Map p 81.*

Gifts & Viennese Souvenirs

★★★ **Duft und Kultur** CITY CENTER   A fragrant treasure trove with an unusual combination of witty gift ideas, luxury toiletries, costume jewelry, scented candles, vases, and exotic oriental artifacts. *Tuchlauben 17.* ☎ *01 532 3960. AE, DC, MC, V. U-Bahn 1/3 (Stephansplatz). Map p 82.*

★ **Petit Point** CITY CENTER   Fine *petit point* inspired by the embroidery of Viennese court ladies during the rococo era. Delicate evening bags and brooches make classic souvenirs. *Hofburgpassage 2.* ☎ *01 533 6098. AE, DC, MC, V. www.maria-stransky.at. U-Bahn 3 (Herrengasse). Map p 81.*

★★ **Swarovski** CITY CENTER   The glittering crystal vases, jewelry, and accessories produced by this celebrated Tyrolean glass-maker enjoy an international reputation. Kids especially love the distinctive miniature animals. *Kärntnerstrasse 8.* ☎ *01 903 3233. www.swarovski.com. AE, DC, MC, V. U-Bahn 1/3 (Stephansplatz).*

Jewelry

★ **Elisabeth Krainer** CITY CENTER   Tucked away in a small courtyard, this workshop welcomes visitors to watch the production of elegant, vivid jewelry using a wide variety of precious stones. *Tuchlauben 17 (Innenhof).* ☎ *01 522 0633. www.krainerschmuck.at. AE, DC, MC, V. U-Bahn 1/3 (Stephansplatz). Map p 82.*

★★★ **Frey Wille** CITY CENTER   Distinctive gold jewelry, scarves, ties, and cufflinks with striking designs in luminous enamel colors, inspired by artists such as Monet, Klimt, and Hundertwasser. *Lobkowitzplatz 1.* ☎ *01 513 8009–14. www.frey-wille.com. AE, DC, MC, V. Tram D/J/1/2 (Oper). Map p 81.*

★★ **Schullin** CITY CENTER   The unusual modern wood-and-marble façade of this family-run jeweler reflects the contemporary design and quality craftsmanship on display inside. *Kohlmarkt 7.* ☎ *01 533 9007. www.schullin.com. AE, DC, MC, V. U-Bahn 3 (Herrengasse). Map p 82.*

Museum Shops

★★★ **Albertina** CITY CENTER   This expansive museum shop stocks an artistic A–Z of quality Viennese souvenirs plus a superb choice of

Snow Globes

Vienna is the home of the snow globe, invented by Erwin Perzy in 1890. The cheap, mass-produced imitations found elsewhere may seem no more than tourist kitsch, but those made here in Vienna's Hernals district are lovingly crafted by hand. The original company (now run by Perzy's grandson) makes over 200,000 snow globes a year. A small museum at the factory displays some of the myriad designs. *Schumanngasse 87.* ☎ *01 486 4341. www.viennasnowglobe.at. No credit cards. Mon–Thurs 9am–3pm. Tram 42 (Antonigasse).*

Schulin's unusual façade was designed by Hans Hollein.

art history and coffee-table books. *Albertinaplatz 1.* ☎ *01 534 83–552. www.albertina.at. AE, MC, V. Tram D/J/1/2 (Oper). Map p 81.*

★★★ Belvedere Museum

BELVEDERE Presents inspired by Klimt and his peers dominate this gift shop. It's also great for kids' gifts, as well as posters, scarves, calendars, and ties. *Prinz-Eugen-Strasse 27.* ☎ *01 795 57–0. www.belvedere. at. AE, DC, MC, V. Tram D (Schloss Belvedere). Map p 84.*

★★ MUMOK MQ This shop is

crammed with eccentric goodies and amusing presents for all the

family—such as paper vases, mobiles, puzzles, and doodle books—as befits a trendy, modern art gallery. *Museumsplatz 1.* ☎ *01 52500. www.mumok.at. AE,DC, MC, V. U-Bahn 2 (Museumsquartier). Map p 84.*

★★★ MAK Design Shop CITY

CENTER Even if you don't visit the museum, it's worth coming here for the latest Austrian lifestyle trends, and to pick up some special-edition pieces by local designers. *Stuben-ring 5.* ☎ *01 711 36228. www.mak designshop.at. AE, DC, MC, V. U-Bahn 3 (Stubentor). Map p 82.*

Music

★★ Arcadia RINGSTRASSE Under

the arcades of the State Opera House, this music store contains a wide assortment of quality opera, ballet and classical recordings, books, and musical memorabilia. *Kärtner-strasse 40.* ☎ *01 513 9568. www. arcadia.at. AE, DC, MC, V. Tram 1/2/D/J (Oper).*

★★ Musikhaus Doblinger CITY

CENTER One of Europe's largest specialist shops for sheet music, specialist books, and magazines covering all musical genres from classical to rock and pop. *Dorotheer-gasse 10.* ☎ *515 03–0. www. doblinger.at. AE, DC, MC, V. U-Bahn 1/3 (Stephansplatz).* ●

You'll come across plenty of music themed souvenirs.

5 The Great Outdoors

Stadtpark

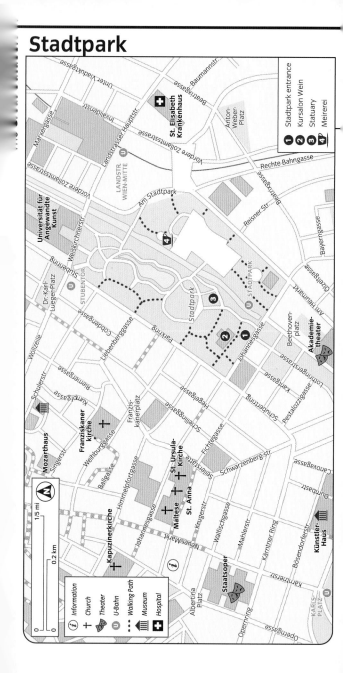

Legend	
ⓘ	Information
✝	Church
◤	Theater
Ⓤ	U-Bahn
⋯	Walking Path
🏛	Museum
✚	Hospital

- ❶ Stadtpark entrance
- ❷ Kursalon Wein
- ❸ Statuary
- ❹ Meirerei

J ust outside the Ringstrasse, the 'City Park' was once open
ground outside the city walls. Flanking the River Wien, it was laid
out in English landscape style in 1862. With its expansive lawns,
shaded areas, playground, and duck pond, it is a popular and tranquil
destination for tourists and locals alike just on the fringe of the inner
city (although it is best avoided after dark). START: **U-Bahn 4 (Stadtpark).**

*The Kursalon—the place to hear Strauss
waltzes.*

**❶ ★★★ kids Stadtpark
entrance.** The main entrance
(off Johannesgasse) is flanked by
magnificent Jugendstil portals of
carved stone. The chase scene
through the sewers at the end of *The
Third Man* movie—one of the most
famous in the history of cinema—
was produced under the bridge here.
See p 51.

❷ ★ Kursalon Wien. *See p 137.*

❸ ★ Statuary. Scattered around
the park you'll find busts commemo-
rating some of the many musicians
and artists associated with Vienna—
Schubert, Bruckner, and Lehár are
here, together with landscape
painter, Emil Schindler (1842–92) and
the hugely influential artist, designer,
and 'magician of colors', Hans
Makart (1840–84). The park's most
famous tenant, however, is Johann
Strauss II. The rather tacky, gilded
statue of the 'King of the Waltz' playing his violin near the Kursalon is
without doubt Vienna's most famous
(and much photographed) statue.

❹ ★★ Meirerei. This riverside
'milkbar' café, with trendy white-
on-white décor (adjoining the
celebrated gourmet restaurant
Steireck), serves superb breakfasts, light snacks, 120 different
cheeses, and traditional Austrian
desserts. *Am Heumarkt 2.* ☎ *01
713 3168. $$.*

Kids' Playgrounds

Viennese playgrounds are generally excellent, featuring plenty
of sturdy swings, slides, sandpits, and tree-houses. The Stadtpark
has one of the best. Others can be found beside Karlskirche, in the
Rathauspark, at Börseplatz and, further afield, at Schlichplatz (in
Alsergrund) and Schönborn Park (in Josefstadt). The Prater has sev-
eral wonderful playgrounds too (see p 97). The Schönbrunn Park's
Irrgarten ('Crazy Garden', see p 108, bullet ❺) is the most eccentric,
but most parents like the one at the University campus best, as it's
right next to a beer-garden.

Prater

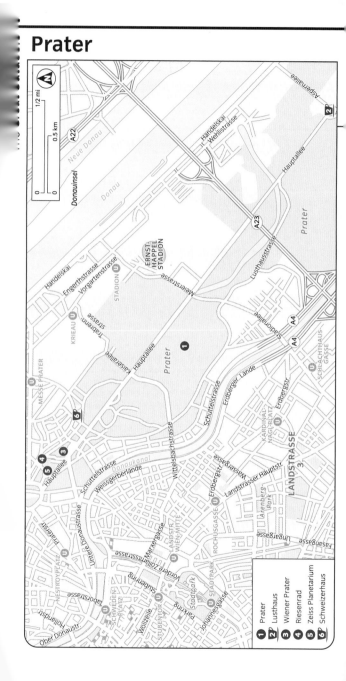

1 Prater
2 Lusthaus
3 Wiener Prater
4 Riesenrad
5 Zeiss Planetarium
6 Schweizerhaus

On sunny days, all year round, there's nothing I enjoy more than strolling in this vast and famous park alongside the Danube. Here you can wander at will past the Wiener Prater amusement park with its famous giant ferris wheel, through woodland and vast sunbathing meadows to one of its fine beer-gardens. This is undoubtedly one of the best places in the city to watch the Viennese at play.

1 ★★★ kids Prater. In 1766, Josef II opened the old imperial hunting grounds to the public, creating a huge tract of recreational parkland. The Prater is now Vienna's most popular park and one of its main 'green lungs', criss-crossed by a maze of quiet paths and streams which meander through open fields and mixed woodland. The less-lit parts of the park are best avoided after dark, however, as the Prater is a well-known hotspot for petty crime. It is a major sporting venue, containing the Ernst Happel football stadium (venue of the Euro2008 football tournament) and a trotting stadium, which stages international trotting races from September through June. Its golf course, tennis courts, and swimming pool appeal to sports enthusiasts, while kids love the vast open spaces for picnics, games, and tree-climbing. It has well-equipped playgrounds, skateboard and BMX courses for older children, pony-riding (on the fringes of the Wurstelprater), and even a mini-train (the Liliput-Bahn) which tours the park every 30 minutes from 10am–7pm (from the Riesenrad). You can hire a bike or some rollerblades (see Bike Rentals, p 162) or take a small boat on the Heustadlwasser. A broad avenue (known as the Hauptallee), planted with ancient chestnut trees, represents the park's backbone, stretching 5km (3 miles) from the idyllic Green Prater to the Wurstelprater funfair zone. *U-Bahn 3 (Erdberg)/U-Bahn 2 (Ernst Happel Stadion). www.prater.at.*

The Lusthaus restaurant was once an imperial hunting lodge.

2 ★★ Lusthaus. This unusual 18th-century octagonal pavilion at the heart of the Prater woods was originally built as a hunting lodge. Now converted to a restaurant, it retains its imperial dignity and is a popular choice with locals for special occasions. Try the game dishes in season—the version with fresh herbs and cranberries is especially tasty. *Freudenau 254.* ☎ *01 728 9565. $$–$$$.*

3 ★ kids Wiener Prater. At the western end of the Prater, you can travel on a ghost train, ride an old-fashioned merry-go-round or drive a

High-adrenalin action at the Wiener Prater.

100-year-old structure was built by an Englishman named Walter Basset, and is one of the city's great landmarks, immortalized in the movie *The Third Man*. It takes 20 minutes to complete one circuit and is especially magical (and therefore often busier) at night. As well as the ride there's also a charming small museum in the entrance area, which illustrates the history of the wheel and the city in miniature—all contained within some of the Riesenrad's old red cabins. For a really special occasion, you can hire out a cabin for a romantic dinner or drinks. *Wurstelprater.* ☎ *01 729 5430. www.wienerriesenrad.com. €8 adults, €3.20 kids, €20 family card. Jan–Feb 10am–7pm, Mar–Apr 24, Oct 10am–9.45pm, Apr 25–Sept 9am–11.45pm, Nov–Dec 10am–7.45pm. U-Bahn 1 (Praterstern).*

There's plenty to amuse the kids at the Prater.

dodgem car at the Wurstelprater—the world's oldest amusement park. In the 19th century, it consisted of a few inns, coffee houses, badminton courts, a bowling alley, and a ferris wheel, built to amuse the Viennese working classes. Now, with over 250 hi-tech rides, sideshows, and fast-food stands, it's one of Vienna's top leisure attractions—a colorful, noisy spectacle for all the family. Don't miss the watery Donau-Jump; the revolting Dizzy Mouse; or the high-octane Volare roller-coaster for the ultimate adrenalin rush. ☎ *01 728 0516. www.prater.at. Free admission; rides cost between €1–€10. Mar 15–Oct 10am–midnight. U-Bahn 1 (Praterstern).*

④ ★★★ kids Riesenrad. My favorite ride at the Wurstelprater funfair is undoubtedly atop the world-famous Riesenrad, or ferris wheel. Gliding slowly to a height of 67m above the rooftops, you catch awesome views of Vienna, UNO City (see p 101, bullet ⑥), and the Wienerwald beyond. This giant

A Danube tourist boat passes the Franz-von-Assisi-Kirche.

5 ★ **kids** Zeiss Planetarium.
The state-of-the-art Zeiss projector enables budding astronomers to star-gaze into the skies above the Prater—over 9,000 stars are visible on a clear night—or to enjoy one of the exciting film shows, which are geared towards a young audience. *Oswald Thomas-Platz 1.* ☎ *01 729 5494. www.planetarium-wien.at.* €8 *adults,* €6 *kids. Phone for show times. U-Bahn 1 (Praterstern).*

6 ★★★ **kids** Schweizerhaus.
There's always a lively crowd in this enormous beer-garden, which seats 1,300 people. Try the specialty crispy *Stelzen* (pigs' trotters), or one of several other authentic Bohemian specialities, all washed down by the best Czech Budvar beer in town. *Strasse des ersten Mai 116.* ☎ *01 728 0152. $$. Mid-Mar–Oct Mon–Sat 10am–11.30pm).*

Danube Boat Trips

The longer Danube cruises offered by the Blue Danube Shipping riverboats pass some of the finest river scenery in Europe. A summer day tour into the wine country of Austria's Wachau region (with time to visit Melk's impressive baroque abbey) is especially scenic. Visit the Slovakian capital, Bratislava, just 1¼ hours away by high-speed catamaran (five sailings daily, Apr–Sept). Or take a half-day trip (daily departures 9am from Salztorbrücke, May–Sept) to explore the Lobau National Park—a beautiful, unspoilt wetland area with exceptional flora and fauna just outside the city, and a must for nature lovers (y 01 4000 49 480 for details).

The **Danube**

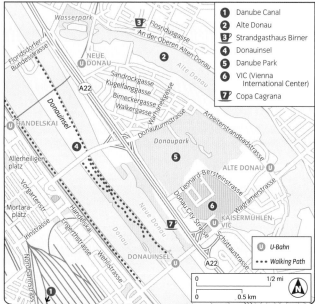

1. Danube Canal
2. Alte Donau
3. Strandgasthaus Birner
4. Donauinsel
5. Danube Park
6. VIC (Vienna International Center)
7. Copa Cagrana

🔵 *U-Bahn*
••• *Walking Path*

I love the majestic River Danube (known as the Donau in Vienna), even if it isn't strictly blue, as Strauss's celebrated waltz insists. Its status as a major European waterway is indisputable, flowing 2,860km from Germany's Black Forest through Austria to the Black Sea. Yet in Vienna it simply offers a huge recreational area in which to relax, sunbathe, sail, and swim—all just a stone's throw from the city center.

❶ ★★★ kids Danube Canal cruise. *See p 22, bullet ❷.*

❷ ★★★ kids Alte Donau. The 'Old Danube' carried the main flow of the river until 1875 when its course was changed to prevent flooding, turning it into a vast, landlocked expanse of water. Ever since, it has been a favorite destination for Viennese bathers and boating enthusiasts. The largest and most popular of several beach complexes here is Gänsehäufel (Goose Island),

which has kids' pools, water slides, beach volleyball, cafés, playgrounds, and mini-golf. *Alte Donau:* 🕐 *2hr. U-Bahn 1 (Alte Donau). Gänsehäufel: Moissigasse 21.* ☎ *01 269 9016. www.gaensehaeufel.at. Daily (May–Sept only): Mon–Fri 9am–8pm, Sat–Sun 8am–8pm. €4.50 adults (€3.50 for half-day), € 1.50 kids (€1.50 half-day). U-Bahn 1 (Kaisermühlen), then free Bäderbus (baths bus) every 15 minutes from the U-Bahn to the beach (late May–Aug).*

3 ★★★ **Strandgasthaus Birner.**
Little has changed since this old-fashioned beach restaurant on the Alte Donau opened in the 1930s. It has a sunny riverside terrace, superb fish specialties, and traditional Viennese cuisine. *Obere Alte Donau 47.* 01 271 53 36. *$$.*

4 ★★ kids **Donauinsel.** The Danube Island was created in the 1980s when the Neue Donau (New Danube) was constructed parallel to the main river to prevent flooding. Criss-crossed by paths and with over 40km of *Schotterstrände* (gravel beaches), this tiny sliver of land is a paradise for cyclists, walkers and sunbathers, with bikes, inline skates and boats to hire. The tips of the island are designated nudist zones. In late June the island hosts the hugely popular Donauinselfest—a three-day festival of rock, pop, and folk music which draws up to 3 million fans annually. *1hr. www.donauinsel.at, www.donauinselfest.at. U-Bahn 1 (Donauinsel).*

5 ★★ kids **Danube Park.**
Vienna's second-largest park was laid out in 1964 for the first Vienna International Garden Show. Located on

The Donauinsel is popular with cyclists.

the site of a former military parade ground called Kagran, it is much loved by locals for its maze of cycle lanes and footpaths, rose-garden, playgrounds, giant chess, mini-train, open-air theater, beaches, and petting zoo. Vienna's tallest structure, the Donauturm (Danube Tower) rises 252m above the park. Whizz up the lift on a clear day to admire the sweeping vistas extending as far as Hungary and the Alps. There's a revolving café and restaurant at the top. *2hr. Donauturmstrasse 4.* 01 263 3572. *www.donauturm.at. Daily 10am–midnight. €5.50 adults, €4.10 kids. U-Bahn 1 (Kaisermühlen).*

6 ★ **Vienna International Center (VIC).** This ultra-modern cluster of Y-shaped skyscrapers is home to numerous international organizations. It serves as one of the United Nations' four headquarters (along with New York, Geneva, and Nairobi), hence its local nickname 'UNO City'. Take a guided tour for a rare insight into the varied work of the UN. Boats can be hired at Eppel Boote (Wagramer Strasse 48a) or Kukis Kombüse (Wagramerstrasse 48d). *tours last one hour; you need a passport to get in. Wagramerstrasse 5.* 01 260 60-3328. *www.unvienna.org. €5 adults, €3 concessions, €2 kids. Mon–Fri 11am and 2pm (also 12.30pm from June–Aug). U-Bahn 1 (Kaisermühlen/Vienna International Center).*

7 ★ **Copa Cagrana.** It's party time all summer long at the exotic cafés, bars, and clubs of UNO City's Copa Cagrana complex (this strip was once known as Kagran and is now amusingly named after Rio's Copacabana Beach). Although some of the eateries here are a little tacky, it's worth checking out the Greek-style Taverne Sokrates (0650 587 4111, $) or romantic Fisch + Mehr (0650 535 9224, $$).

Grinzing

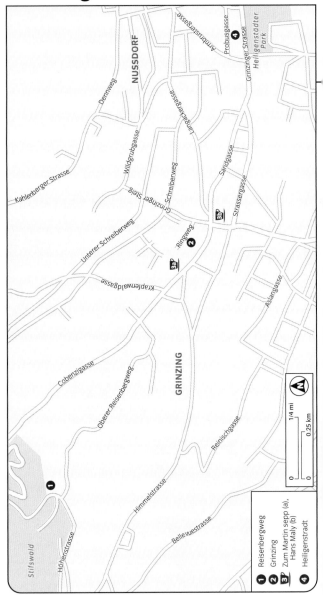

1 Reisenbergweg
2 Grinzing
3 Zum Martin sepp (a),
Hans Maly (b)
4 Heiligenstradt

In the northwestern outskirts of Vienna lies a region of picturesque old wine villages and vineyard-striped hills. This is where the prestigious Grüner Veltliner white wines are produced. Grinzing is one of the best-known and popular wine villages, noted for its quaint old houses and *gemütlich* (cosy) wine taverns, or *Heurigen*, usually marked by a bunch or wreath of pine sprigs. **START: Cobenzl Parkplatz (U-Bahn 4 (Heiligenstadt) then bus 38a (Cobenzl Parkplatz)).**

❶ ★★★ kids Reisenbergweg. On arrival at Cobenzl (450m), pause awhile to admire the breathtaking views over Vienna (there's a coffee house and petting farm here too). Cross the road and descend a narrow country lane (Oberer Reisenbergweg) through the vineyards to the village of Grinzing, stopping for your first tipple of local wine at Weingut am Reisenberg (Thurs–Sat 5pm–11pm, Sun 1pm–11pm (9pm in winter)) halfway down. Mozart wrote to his father in 1781 'I live just one hour away from Vienna. It's called Reisenberg and it's very pleasant here'! *Bus 38a (Cobenzl Parkplatz).*

❷ ★★★ Grinzing. Grinzing has preserved its charming village

The view from the Reisenbergweg.

Each Heurige has its own crest.

character, despite the large number of tourists who frequent its numerous *Heurigen*. Most of the romantic old vintners' houses date from the 16th and 17th centuries. Grinzing has many associations with historical celebrities: Schubert wrote some of his songs on local outings, and Strauss composed his *Tales from the Vienna Woods* nearby. The secret of dreams was revealed to Freud here, and Mahler is buried in the village cemetery. *Bus 38a (Grinzing).*

❸ ★★★ Two of my favorite *Heurigen* lie close together. **Zum Martin Sepp** (Cobenzlgasse 34, ☎ 01 320 3233, $$) has a jolly courtyard garden and serves nourishing bar meals. **Hans Maly** (Sandgasse 8, ☎ 01 320 1384, $) also has a picturesque garden, but serves simpler fare. Like many *Heurigen*, both often offer live music. They are less touristy out of season.

❹ ★★ Heiligenstadt. Beethoven spent a number of summers in Heiligenstadt, hoping that the country air would alleviate his deafness. You can visit one of his apartments (Probusgasse 6, ☎ 01 370 5408, Tues–Sun 10am–1pm, 2pm–6pm). Nearby, rustic **Mayer am Pfarrplatz** is one of Vienna's top *Heurigen* (Pfarrplatz 2, ☎ 01 370 1287, $$). *Bus 38A (Fernsprechamt).*

Schönbrunn

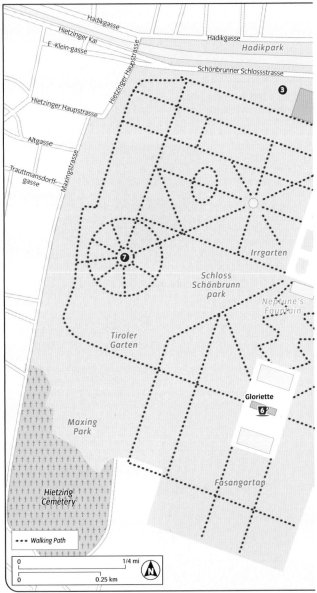

Hadikgasse

Hietzinger Kai

E.-Klein-gasse

Hadikgasse

Hadikpark

Hietzinger Haupstrasse

Schönbrunner Schlossstrasse

❸

Hietzinger Haupstrasse

Altgasse

Maxingstrasse

Trauttmansdorff-gasse

❼

Irrgarten

Schloss Schönbrunn park

Neptune's Fountain

Tiroler Garten

Gloriette

❻

Maxing Park

Fasangartan

Hietzing Cemetery

- - - Walking Path

0   1/4 mi

0   0.25 km

N

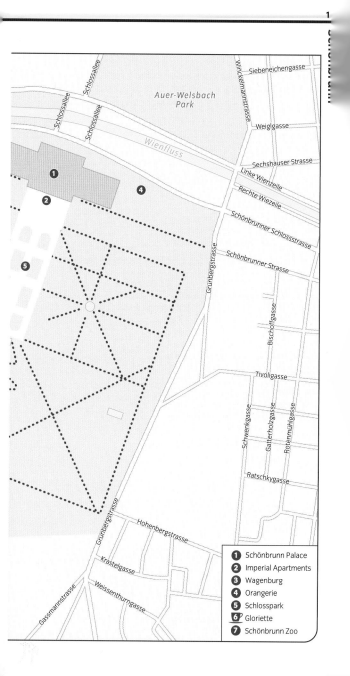

1 Schönbrunn Palace
2 Imperial Apartments
3 Wagenburg
4 Orangerie
5 Schlosspark
6 Gloriette
7 Schönbrunn Zoo

What Versailles is to France, Schönbrunn is to Austria. This grandiose baroque palace was once the summer residence of the imperial family. It is hard to believe that it began life as a simple hunting lodge, built by Maximilian II in 1569, taking its name from the 'beautiful spring' found here. Now listed as a UNESCO World Heritage Site, it is Vienna's most-visited historic building.

1 ★★★ **kids** **Schönbrunn Palace.** Leopold I commissioned the great architect Fischer von Erlach to build a monumental palace here for his son in the 17th century. It remained incomplete until Empress Maria Theresa added another floor to accommodate her 16 children, supervised the interior design and the layout of the grounds, and painted it her favorite color—*Schönbrunnergelb* (Schönbrunn yellow). *See bullet* **2**.

2 ★★★ **Imperial Apartments.** Maria Theresa is the monarch most closely associated with the palace. She lived here with her entourage of 1,500 staff and courtiers. The state rooms with their extravagant rococo décor give an evocative insight into her lifestyle. Of the two guided tours on offer, choose the 'Grand Tour' which visits 40 rooms (out of nearly 2,000 in total)—the Imperial Tour covers only 22 rooms, not including the impressive west wing.

3 ★ **Wagenburg.** It is fun to wind the clocks back to olden times at the Imperial Carriage Collection, with its magnificent horse-drawn carriages, sedan chairs, and fairy-tale sleighs housed in the Winter Riding School. 🕐 *30min. Schönbrunner Schlossstrasse.* 📞 *01 525 24–0. www.khm.at. €4.50 adults, €3/€3.60 concessions, €2.50 kids, €9 family. Daily Apr–Oct 9am–6pm, Nov–Mar Tues–Sun 10am–4pm. U-Bahn 4 (Schönbrunn).*

4 ★ **Orangerie im Schloss Schönbrunn.** This grand 18th-century edifice is the world's second-largest baroque orangery after Versailles. Part of it is still used to over-winter citrus trees. The other section hosts nightly Mozart and Strauss concerts, performed by the Schönbrunn Palace Orchestra. In

Schoenbrunn Palace—Vienna's most visited attraction.

Imperial Apartments

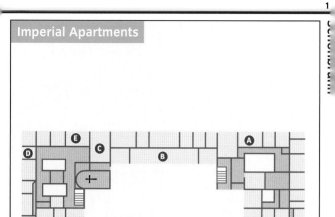

† Church

▨ Stairs to next floor

The tour starts in the private rooms of Elisabeth (Sisi) and Franz Josef. A highlight of the state apartments is the **2A** ★★ **Hall of Mirrors,** where the six-year-old Mozart first played the clavichord to Maria Theresa in 1762. His virtuoso performance was soon the talk of the town, laying the foundations for his meteoric rise to fame. The **2B** ★★ **Great Gallery** is dominated by three enormous ceiling frescoes celebrating the glory of the Habsburgs, and illuminated by magnificent chandeliers. In the painting of Isabella's wedding procession in **2C** ★ **Hall of Ceremonies,** each of the 98 coaches belonging to the aristocracy of Europe is identifiable by its family insignia. Maria Theresa clearly had expensive tastes; she spent a million silver florins on the rosewood paneling and priceless miniatures in the **2D** ★★★ **Million Room.** Finally, don't miss the **2E** ★★ **Blue Chinese Room** where Karl I abdicated in 1918, ending a remarkable six centuries of Habsburg rule. ⏱ *2hr. Early morning is very busy; lunchtime is the quietest time to visit. Schönbrunner Schlossstrasse.* ☎ *01 811 13–239. www.schoenbrunn.at. Grand Tour (40 rooms)/Imperial Tour (22 rooms): €12.90/€9.50 adults, €11.40/€8.50 concessions, €7.90/€5.90 kids (6–18). Apr–Oct 8.30am–5pm (6pm July–Aug), Nov–Mar 8.30am–4.30pm. U-Bahn 4 (Schloss Schönbrunn).*

this setting in 1785, Mozart and his lifelong adversary Antonio Salieri vied for supremacy in a composers' competition (one of the most memorable scenes in the movie *Amadeus*). In case you're wondering . . . Salieri won. *Schönbrunner Schlossstrasse.* ☎ *01 812 5004–0. www.image vienna.com. Tickets (€39–€75) available online. U-Bahn 4 (Schönbrunn).*

5 ★★★ **kids** **Schlosspark.** It's hard not to feel rather superior as you stroll among the statues, fountains, immaculately clipped hedging, and bright flower-filled beds of the vast and beautiful Palace Park. Laid out by Maria Theresa's son, Joseph II (a keen gardener), in the strict symmetry of French-style gardens of the era, it's a wonderful place to watch the Viennese at leisure. The grandest follies in the park include the Schöner Brunnen (beautiful fountain) after which the palace is named, complete with grotto and nymph in true baroque style; the Fountain of Neptune facing the palace; and the majestic Gloriette—a neoclassical arcade. The magnificent iron-and-glass Palm House (a replica of the one in London's Kew Gardens), is full of exotic plants collected over centuries. A Desert House contains plants from arid regions. Kids large and small will love the Maze and the adjoining Irrgarten (Crazy Garden)—an eccentric kids' playground full of unusual wooden toys, crazy mirrors, sandpits, and wacky climbing frames. ⏱ *2hr. Schlosspark.* ☎ *No phone. www.schoenbrunn.at. Free admission. Apr–Oct 6am–dusk; Nov–Mar 6.30am–dusk (phone for exact times). Palm House: €4 adults, €2 kids. Daily 9.30am–5pm. Maze/ Irrgarten: €2.90 adults, €1.70 kids, €5.80 family ticket. Apr–June, Sept 9am–6pm; July–Aug 9am–7pm; Oct 9am–5pm. U-Bahn (Schönbrunn).*

Children just love the Palace's Irrgarten ('Crazy Garden').

upmarket café affords sensational views, especially at sunset. *Schlosspark.* ☎ *01 879 1311. $$.*

7 ★★★ **kids** **Schönbrunn Zoo.** Take a break from all the art, music, and culture, and visit the zoo— Vienna's most-visited attraction after Schönbrunn Palace. It's the oldest zoo in the world, founded in 1752 by Emperor Franz I. Some of the 750-plus animals are housed in original baroque buildings. You can travel round the enclosures by minitrain. Current crowd-pullers include a set of polar bear twins and Fu Long the panda, all born in 2007. ⏱ *2hr. Avoid weekends and school holidays if possible. Maxingstrasse 13b.* ☎ *01 877 9294. www.zoo vienna.at. €12 adults, €5 kids & concessions (free under 5). Feb 9am–5pm, Mar 9am–5.30pm, Apr– Sept 9am–6.30pm, Oct–Jan 9am– 4.30pm. U-Bahn 4 (Hietzing).* ●

6 ★★ **Gloriette.** This immense neoclassical arcade was built to commemorate the Austro-Hungarian victory over the Prussians in 1775. Sited high on a hill overlooking the palace and gardens, with the city as a distant backdrop, its

Dining Best Bets

Most **Eccentric Loos**
★★ Steirerek, *Am Stadtpark (p 121)*

Best **Noodle Bar**
★★★ Ra'mien, *Gumpendorfer-strasse 9 (p 120)*

Best for **Carnivores**
★ Ribs of Vienna, *Weihburggasse 22 (p 120)*

Best for **Afternoon Tea and Cake**
★★★ Café Sacher, *Philharmoniker-strasse 4 (p 117)*

Best **Wiener Schnitzel**
★★★ Figlmüller, *Wollzeile 5 (see p 10, bullet* **2** *) (p 8)*

Best **Neighborhood Italian**
★★★ Osteria Numero Uno, *Burggasse 25 (p 120)*

Best **Boho Café**
★★ Hawelka, *Dorotheergasse 6 (p 118)*

Most **Traditional Coffeehouse**
★★★ Café Sperl, *Gumpendorfer-strasse 11 (p 117)*

Best **Fish**
★★ Lobsterdock, *Karlsplatz 5 (p 119)*

Best **Ice-Cream**
★★★ Zanoni & Zanoni, *Lugeck 7 (p 121)*

Best **Asian Cuisine**
★★ Indochine 21, *Stubenring 18 (p 118)*

Best **Brunch**
★★★ Naschmarkt Deli, *Naschmarkt 421-436 (p 120)*

Best **Beer Cellar for a Meal**
★★★ Zwölf Apostelkeller, *Sonnen-felsgasse 3 (p 122)*

Best **Museum Café**
★★★ Milo, *Museumsplatz 1 (p 120)*

Best **Alfresco Meal**
★★★ Witwe Bolte, *Gutenberggasse 13 (p 121)*

Best **Bohemian Cuisine**
★★★ Zu den 3 Buchteln, *Wehrgasse 9 (p 122)*

Café Sperl—one of the oldest and most popular coffeehouses in town.

Dining **Neubau & Naschmarkt**

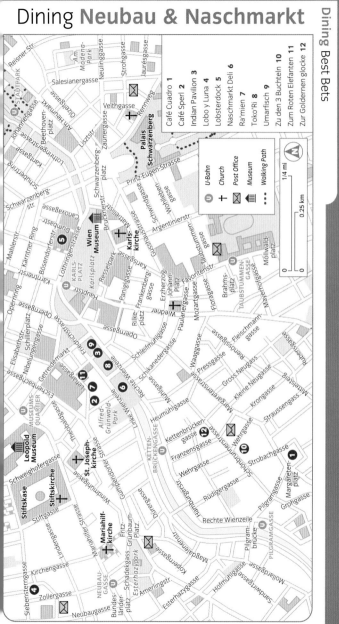

Café Cuadro **1**
Café Sperl **2**
Indian Pavilion **3**
Lobo y Luna **4**
Lobsterdock **5**
Naschmarkt Deli **6**
Ra'mien **7**
Toko'Ri **8**
Umarfisch **9**
Zu den 3 Buchteln **10**
Zum Roten Elefanten **11**
Zur Goldernen glocke **12**

U U-Bahn
+ Church
⊠ Post Office
🏛 Museum
⋯ Walking Path

1/4 mi
0.25 km

Dining **City Center**

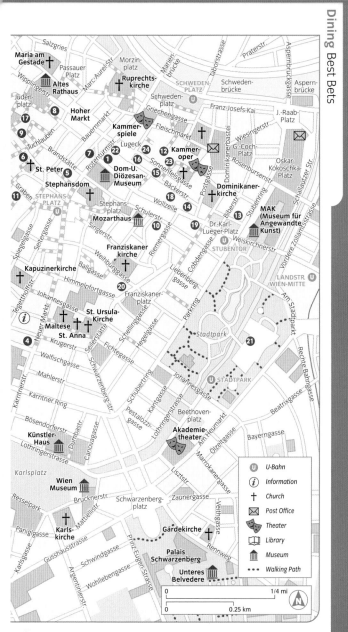

Maria am Gestade †
Passauer Platz
Salzgries
Wipplingerstr.
Marc-Aurel-Str.
Morzin-platz
Marien-brücke
Praterstr.
Aspernbrückgasse
Altes Rathaus
Ruprechts-kirche
SCHWEDEN-PLATZ
Schweden-platz
Schweden-brücke
Aspern-brücke
Juden-platz
Hoher Markt
Griechengasse
Franz-Josefs-Kai
J.-Raab-Platz
8
17
9
Tuchlauben
Bauernmarkt
Kammer-spiele
Fleischmarkt
Wiesingerstr.
G.-Coch-Platz
Oskar-Kokoschka-Platz
Schallautzer Str.
6
St. Peter †
Brandstätte
7
Rotenturmstr.
22
Lugeck
16
24
12 Kammer-oper
23
Dominikanerbastei
Rosenburgenstr.
Stephansdom
1
Dom-U. Diözesan-Museum
15
Sonnenfelsgasse
Bäckerstr.
Postgasse
Biberstr.
11
Graben
STEPHANS-PLATZ
†
Stephansplatz
18
14
Wollzeile
Dominikaner-kirche †
13
MAK (Museum für Angewandte Kunst)
Schulerstr.
Mozarthaus
10
Dr.-Karl-Lueger-Platz
Vordere Zollamtsstrasse
Spiegelgasse
Seilergasse
Singerstr.
Franziskaner-kirche †
Weihburggasse
19
Riemergasse
STUBENTOR
Weiskirchnerstr.
LANDSTR. WIEN-MITTE
Am Stadtpark
Kapuzinerkirche †
Tegetthoffstr.
Himmelpfortgasse
Ballgasse
20
Franziskaner-platz
Liebenberg-gasse
Cobdengasse
Parkring
i
Johannesgasse
St. Ursula-Kirche
Stadtpark
Rechte Bahngasse
Neuer Markt
Maltese †
St. Anna †
Krugerstr.
Seilerstätte
Schellinggasse
Hegelgasse
Fichtegasse
21
Kärntnerstr.
Walfischgasse
Schwarzenberg-str.
STADTPARK
Mahlerstr.
Schubertring
Johannesgasse
Kärntner Ring
Karntnerstr.
Bösendorferstr.
Dumbastr.
Canovagasse
Pestalozzi-gasse
Kantgasse
Lothringerstrasse
Beethoven-platz
Am Heumarkt
Beatrixgasse
Künstler-Haus
Lothringerstrasse
Akademie-theater
Olzeltgasse
Bayerngasse
Karlsplatz
Resselpark
Wien Museum
Bruknerstr.
Martiellistr.
Schwarzenberg-platz
Zaunergasse
Lisztstr.
Marrokanergasse
Karls-kirche †
Paniglgasse
Gusshausstrasse
Argentinierstr.
Schwindgasse
Prinz-Eugen-Strasse
Gardekirche †
Rennweg
Veithgasse
Wohllebengasse
Palais Schwarzenberg
Unteres Belvedere

U	U-Bahn
i	Information
†	Church
✉	Post Office
🎭	Theater
📖	Library
🏛	Museum
···	Walking Path

0   1/4 mi
0   0.25 km

N

Dining **City Center West**

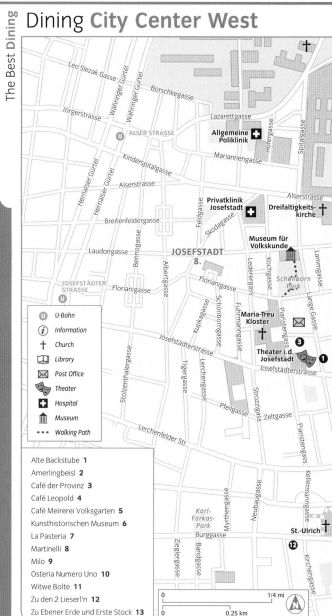

Map Legend

- 🚇 U-Bahn
- ⓘ Information
- † Church
- 📖 Library
- ✉ Post Office
- 🎭 Theater
- ✚ Hospital
- 🏛 Museum
- ••• Walking Path

Alte Backstube **1**

Amerlingbeisl **2**

Café der Provinz **3**

Café Leopold **4**

Café Meirerei Volksgarten **5**

Kunsthistorischen Museum **6**

La Pasteria **7**

Martinelli **8**

Milo **9**

Osteria Numero Uno **10**

Witwe Bolte **11**

Zu den 2 Lieserl'n **12**

Zu Ebener Erde und Erste Stock **13**

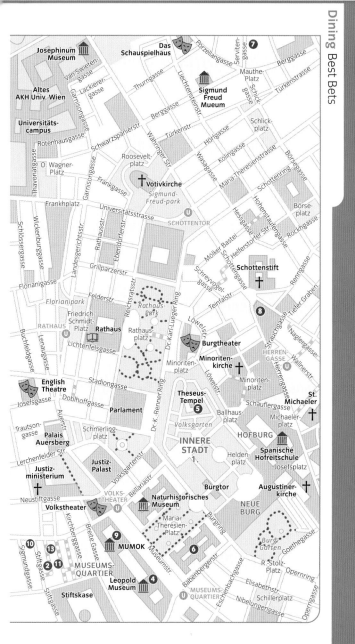

The Best Dining

Vienna Dining A to Z

★ **Akakiko** CITY CENTER ASIAN This trendy chain of Japanese fast-food cafés reflects the city's current craze for exotic cuisine, with sushi, noodle dishes, and bento lunchbox meals to eat in or take out. *Rotenturmstrasse 6.* ☎ *057 333 190. Entrees €8.70–€20.70. MC, V. Lunch & dinner daily. U-Bahn 1/3 (Stephansplatz).*

★★ **Alte Backstube** JOSEFSTADT VIENNESE   Tuck into real Viennese home-cooking in this old-fashioned, country-style, candlelit tavern, housed in a former 17th-century bakery. The lunch menu is especially good. *Lange Gasse 34.* ☎ *01 406 1101. Entrees €13.80–€18.90. MC, V. Lunch & dinner Mon–Sat, dinner Sun. U-Bahn 2 (Rathaus).*

★★ **Augustinerkeller** HOFBURG VIENNESE   Hearty local dishes, beer on tap, and jolly *Heurige* music in the evenings are the order of the day within the ancient brick vaults of this cosy former monastery cellar.

Amerlingbeisl—a true locals' watering-hole.

Augustinerstrasse 1. ☎ *01 533 1026. Entrees €10.90–€22. AE, DC, MC, V. Lunch & dinner daily. Tram 1/2/D/J (Oper).*

★★ **Amerlingbeisl** SPITTELBERG An informal eatery serving simple but varied light bites, including a good vegetarian selection. Sit outside in the pretty, cobbled courtyard. *Stiftgasse 8.* ☎ *01 526 1660. Entrees €6.20–€10.90. AE, DC, MC, V. Breakfast, lunch & dinner daily. Tram 49 (Stiftgasse).*

★★ **Bräunerhof** HOFBURG CAFÉ Join the locals in this genteel tearoom to enjoy a variety of coffees and strudels. At weekends, a quartet plays in the afternoons. *Stallburggasse 2.* ☎ *01 512 3893. Entrees €6.70–10.50. No credit cards. Mon–Fri 8am–9pm, Sat 8am–7pm, Sun, hols 10am–7pm. Tram 1/2/D/J (Oper).*

★★ **kids** **Café Cuadro** MARGARETEN CAFÉ   A trendy organic café, serving bio-breakfasts (until 4pm), square ethno-burgers, salads, vegetarian strudels, and affordable cocktails (from 5pm). *Margaretenstrasse 77.* ☎ *01 544 7550. Entrees €3.90–€9.20. V only. Breakfast, lunch & dinner daily. U-Bahn 4 (Pilgramgasse).*

★ **kids** **Café der Provinz** JOSEFSTADT CAFÉ   This low-key, mellow café draws students and locals to its simple menu of salads, savoury and sweet pancakes, not to mention delicious organic brunches at the weekend. *Maria-Treu-Gasse 3.* ☎ *01 944 2272. €4.80–€7.80. Breakfast, lunch & dinner daily. U-Bahn 2 (Rathaus).*

★★★ **kids** **Café Meirerei Volksgarten** HOFBURG CAFÉ   Come to this tiny garden pavilion for its sensational al fresco buck's fizz breakfasts, gooey gateaux, and ice-cream sundaes. *Volksgarten.* ☎ *01 533 2105. Entrees €3.80–€12.60. AE, DC, MC, V. Breakfast, lunch & dinner daily. U-Bahn 4.*

★★★ **Café Sacher** CITY CENTER CAFÉ *The* place to try Vienna's famous chocolate cake, *Sacher-torte*, made to a secret recipe and served with whipped cream in a posh, traditional tea-room. *Philhar-monikerstrasse 4.* ☎ *01 51 456-0. Entrees €15.60–€19.50. AE, DC, MC, V. Breakfast, lunch & dinner daily. Tram 1/2/D/J (Oper).*

★★★ **Café Sperl** MQ CAFÉ One of Vienna's best-loved cafés, serving local dishes in a plush, *fin-de-siècle* setting. Newspapers and billiard-tables add to the relaxed ambience. *Gumpendorferstrasse 11.* ☎ *01 586 4158. Entrees €7.10–€9.80. AE, DC, MC, V. Mon–Sat 7am–11pm, Sun 11am–8pm (closed Sun in summer). U-Bahn 1/2/4 (Karlsplatz).*

★★★ **Cantinetta Antinori** CITY CENTER ITALIAN Enjoy sophisticated Italian cuisine and top-notch wines al fresco or in a spacious, chande-lier-lit dining-room. Popular for busi-ness lunches. *Jasmirogottstrasse 3/5.* ☎ *01 533 7722. Entrees €20.50–€34. AE, DC, MC, V. Lunch & dinner daily. U-Bahn 1/3 (Stephansplatz).*

★★ **Café Leopold** MQ CAFÉ Hip, arty types frequent the Leopold Museum's cool café-bar for tasty brunches, bagels, and wraps during the day, followed by cocktails and funky DJ sounds at night. *Museum-splatz 1.* ☎ *01 523 6732. Entrees €3.90–€10.50. MC, V. Daily 10am–2am (4am Thurs–Sat). U-Bahn 2 (Museumsquartier).*

★ **Fabios** FREYUNG MEDITER-RANEAN See and be seen in this sophisticated, minimalist retaurant

Café Sperl—the archetypal Viennese coffee house.

where the décor is sleek, the wait-ers suave, and the modern-Mediter-ranean cuisine impeccable. Save room for dessert. *Tuchlauben 6.* ☎ *01 532 2222. Entrees €24–€33.50. AE, DC, MC, V. Lunch & dinner Mon–Sat. U-Bahn 3 (Herrengasse).*

★★ **Fratelli** CITY CENTER ITALIAN Hugely popular Italian restaurant serving home-made pastas and piz-zas. Ask for a table on the lovely shaded terrace or in the wittily fres-coed, brick-vaulted basement. *Roten-turmstrasse 24 (entrance on Ertlplatz).* ☎ *01 533 8745. €7.90–€24.50. AE, DC, MC, V. Lunch & dinner daily. U-Bahn 1/3 (Stephansplatz).*

★ **kids Fresh Soup & Salad** CITY CENTER The simple but tasty home-made soups, curries, and salads at this modern, unfussy café make an ideal lunch-break for shoppers and sightseers. *Wipplingerstrasse 1.* ☎ *0664 857 5871. Entrees €3.90–€5.70. No credit cards. Mon–Fri 11am–7.30pm. Sat 11am–5.30pm. U-Bahn 1/3 (Stephansplatz).*

★★ **kids Kunsthistorisches Museum** MQ CAFÉ Grab a

coffee or a light snack between galleries in the KHM's grand cupola hall. Book in advance for the special Sunday Art and Buffet brunch and art tour. *KHM, Maria-Theresien-Platz.* ☎ *01 526 1361. Entrees €6.90–€9.90. AE, DC, MC, V. Tues–Sun 10am–5pm. Tram 1/2 (Burgring).*

★★ kids Gösser Bierklinik
FREYUNG BEER CELLAR   One of the top drinking haunts in Vienna, this jolly beer cellar—with a level of noise to delight parents of toddlers - serves superb ales and hearty Viennese *Schmankerln* (delicacies), including beer soup. *Steindlgasse 4.* ☎ *01 535 6897. Entrees €7–€18. DC, MC, V. Lunch & dinner Mon–Sat. U-Bahn 1/3 (Stephansplatz).*

★ kids Gulaschmuseum CITY
CENTER AUSTO-HUNGARIAN   Fifteen different types of *gulasch* (a meaty casserole seasoned with paprika) are served here, including even a chocolate *gulasch* for dessert. *Schulerstrasse 20.* ☎ *01 512 1017. Entrees €8–€14. MC, V. Breakfast, lunch & dinner daily. U-Bahn 1/3 (Stephansplatz).*

★★ Hawelka CITY CENTER CAFÉ
This scruffy, bohemian café has long attracted artists and local literati.

Join them here at 10pm when hot *Buchteln* (jam doughnuts) are served. Scrumptious with coffee. *Dorotheergasse 6.* ☎ *01 512 8230. Snacks €3.50–€4.30. No credit cards. Mon, Wed–Sat 8am–2am, Sun 10am–2am. U-Bahn 1/3 (Stephansplatz).*

★★★ Hollmann Salon CITY CEN-
TER AUSTRIAN   This stylish restaurant serves high-quality three- and four-course menus of organic, regional cuisine, and beautifully crafted desserts. *Grashofgasse 3 (entrance in Heiligenkreuzerhof).* ☎ *01 96 11 960–40. Menus €13–€49. AE, DC, MC, V. Lunch & dinner Mon–Sat. U-Bahn 4 (Schwedenplatz).*

★★★ Indian Pavilion
NASCHMARKT INDIAN   Try the specialty *thali* (mixed curry platter) on the pavement terrace of this tiny market café, washed down by Cobra beer, a mango *lassi* (yogurt drink), or Darjeeling tea with cardamom. *Naschmarkt 74-75.* ☎ *01 587 8561. Entrees €9.50–€12.50. No credit cards. Mon–Fri 11am–6.30pm, Sat 11am–5pm. U-Bahn 1/2/4 (Karlsplatz).*

★★ Indochine 21 CITY CENTER
ASIAN   Transport yourself to Indochina via the spicy hotpots, fish dishes, and exotic fruits of this chic restaurant, which specializes in

Indochine 21—the ultimate in French-Vietnamese cuisine.

outstanding modern French–Vietnamese cuisine. *Stubenring 18.* 📞 *01 513 7660. Entrees €23–€35. AE, DC, MC, V. Lunch & dinner daily. Tram 1/2 (Stubentor).*

★ **kids Inigo** CITY CENTER AUSTRIAN This modern locals' café-restaurant serves affordable international cuisine, including plenty of vegetarian choices. The sofas and armchairs add warmth and comfort. *Bäckerstrasse 18.* 📞 *01 512 7451. AE, DC, MC, V. Entrees €5.40–€10.60. Mon–Sat 9.30–midnight, Sun 10am–4pm. U-Bahn 3 (Stubentor).*

★★ **Kaffee Alt Wien** CITY CENTER CAFÉ Simple, boho and nicotine-stained, the nooks and crannies of this friendly, fun café are packed with students, actors, and journalists into the early hours. *Bäckerstrasse 9.* 📞 *01 512 5222. Lunch & dinner daily. Entrees €10. No credit cards. U-Bahn 1/3 (Stephansplatz).*

★★★ **La Pasteria** SERVITEN ITALIAN Each dish is a work of art at this small, modern deli-restaurant. The antipasti and pasta dishes are especially tasty. Ask for a table on the pavement terrace. *Servitengasse 10.* 📞 *01 310 2736. Entrees €10.50–€19.50. V only. Lunch & dinner Mon–Sat. U-Bahn 4 (Rossauer Lände).*

★★ **Little Buddha** CITY CENTER ASIAN Beyond the imposing entrance, this dramatic black-and-red restaurant serves state-of-the-art trans-Asian cuisine to Vienna's chic set. There's also a plush, intimate basement cocktail bar. *Lugeck 1.* 📞 *01 512 1111. Entrees €17–€19. AE, DC, MC, V. Noon–3am daily. U-Bahn 1/3 (Stephansdom).*

★★ **Lobo y Luna** NEUBAU SPANISH There's a tiny restaurant hidden behind the sleek bar here. It serves a select choice of tasty tapas dishes including chorizo in rioja sauce and prawns in garlic. *Mondscheingasse 2.* 📞 *01 944 9966. Entrees €7.50–€11.50. AE, DC, MC, V. Lunch & dinner Mon–Fri, dinner Sat. U3 (Neubaugasse).*

★★ **Lobsterdock** CITY CENTER FISH The sensational clam chowder and seafood platters will appeal to fish fanatics. Right next to the Musikverein, it's handy for pre- or post-concert dinners. *Karlsplatz 5.* 📞 *01 505 3839. Entrees €19.50–€48. DC, MC, V. Lunch & dinner, Mon–Fri, dinner Sat. U-Bahn 1/2/4 (Karlsplatz).*

★★ **Martinelli** FREYUNG ITALIAN Enjoy fine Italian cuisine in this traditional trattoria, or served alfresco in the shady courtyard of an elegant

Kaffee Alt Wien—a cozy locals haunt.

Lobsterdock—the address for shellfish in town.

baroque palace. Excellent wines. *Palais Harrach, Freyung 3.* ☎ *01 533 6721. Entrees €19.50–€24. AE, DC, MC, V. Lunch & dinner daily. U-Bahn 3 (Herrengasse).*

★★★ **Milo** MQ CAFÉ   The best bet in the MuseumsQuartier, with a mouth-watering bistro-style menu, and scrumptious home-made cakes. The geometric tiled ceiling lends the airy, modern café a Moorish feel. *Museumsplatz 1.* ☎ *01 523 6566. No credit cards. Lunch & dinner daily. U-Bahn 2 (Museumsquartier).*

★★★ kids **Naschmarkt Deli** NASCHMARKT CAFÉ   Come here for hearty all-day breakfasts, market-fresh salads, and mighty triple-decker sandwiches. It's also a trendy bar by night. *Naschmarkt 421-436.* ☎ *01 585 0823. Entrees €4.50–€5.50. No credit cards. Breakfast, lunch & dinner daily Mon–Sat. U-Bahn 1/2/4 (Karlsplatz).*

★★ **Ofenloch** FREYUNG VIENNESE This traditional restaurant serves classic Viennese fare with a modern

twist in a series of cosy, romantic dining-rooms. The *Zwiebelrost-braten* (steak heaped with crispy onions) is especially tasty. *Kurrentgasse 8.* ☎ *01 533 8844. Entrees €13.50–€18.50. AE, MC, V. Lunch & dinner Mon–Sat. U-Bahn 1/3 (Stephansplatz).*

★★★ **Osteria Numero Uno** NEUBAU ITALIAN   The owners make you feel like house guests at this tiny, quirky restaurant. There's no menu: Silvia cooks as many courses as you can eat while Luca serves the wines. *Burggasse 25.* ☎ *01 526 0357. Allow €30 for three courses. No credit cards. Dinner Tues–Sat. U-Bahn 2/3 (Volkstheater).*

★★ **Oswald & Kalb** CITY CENTER VIENNESE   A hugely popular *Beisl* (bistro), serving upmarket variations on Viennese cuisine to the city's beautiful people, in a modern, candlelit setting. *Bäckerstrasse 14.* ☎ *01 512 1371. Entrees €12.90–€25.50. AE, DC, MC, V. Lunch & dinner daily. U-Bahn 3 (Stubentor).*

★★ **Plachutta** CITY CENTER VIENNESE   One of the city's finest restaurants, where the local specialty *Tafelspitz* (boiled beef) has been raised to an art form, with 10 cuts of beef to choose from. *Wollzeile 38.* ☎ *01 512 1577. Entrees €15.10–€25.40. AE, DC, MC, V. Lunch & dinner daily. Tram 1/2. U-Bahn 3 (Stubentor).*

★★★ kids **Ra'mien** MQ ASIAN This hip, Asian fast-food joint combines delicious (and often spicy) noodle dishes from China, Vietnam, and Thailand, with minimalist canteen-chic. *Gumpendorferstrasse 9.* ☎ *01 585 4798. Entrees €6.50–€10. AE, DC, MC, V. Lunch & dinner Tues–Sun. U-Bahn 1/2/4 (Karlsplatz).*

★ **Ribs of Vienna** CITY CENTER This dark but lively cellar restaurant

is paradise for carnivores, serving sticky barbeque ribs and juicy steaks. I challenge anyone to complete the specialty 'meter of spare-ribs'. *Weihburggasse 22.* ☎ *01 513 8519. Entrees €11.60–€21. No credit cards. Mon–Fri 11am–3pm, 5pm–midnight. U-Bahn 1/3 (Stephansplatz).*

★★ Steirerek im Stadtpark

STADTPARK MODERN AUSTRIAN Viennese gossip magazines always feature celebrity diners at this upscale riverside restaurant, long ranked Austria's top gourmet temple. The restrooms count among Europe's quirkiest. *Am Stadtpark.* ☎ *01 713 3168. Entrees €22–€45. AE, DC, MC, V. Lunch & dinner Mon–Fri. U-Bahn 4 (Stadtpark).*

★ kids TokoRi NASCHMARKT

ASIAN There's a friendly, studenty atmosphere at this informal sushi restaurant at the heart of the Naschmarkt. It's ideal for a swift, cheap lunch. *Naschmarkt 261-277.* ☎ *01 587 2616. €7.10–€15.90. MC, V. Lunch & dinner Mon–Sat. U-Bahn 1/2/4 (Karlsplatz).*

Enjoy the informal ambiance of this trendy noodle bar.

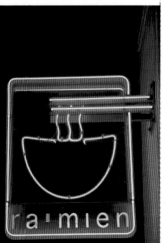

★★ Umarfisch NASCHMARKT

FISH It's worth squeezing round the tiny tables at this Mediterranean-style fish market-café, as it serves the freshest fish and shellfish in town. *Naschmarkt 76-79.* ☎ *01 587 0456. Entrees €18.90–€24. DC, MC, V. Lunch & dinner Mon–Sat. U-Bahn 1/2/4 (Karlsplatz).*

★★★ Witwe Bolte SPITTELBERG

AUSTRIAN Enjoy classic regional dishes, fish, game and steaks at this tiny, traditional locale, or on its beautiful tree-shaded terrace in a fountain-splashed, cobbled square. *Gutenberggasse 13.* ☎ *01 523 1450. Entrees €15.20–€23. AE, DC, MC, V. Lunch & dinner daily. U-Bahn 2/3 (Volkstheater).*

★★★ kids Zanoni & Zanoni

CITY CENTER ICE-CREAM PARLOUR Over 50 different ice-cream flavors await you at this popular *gelateria*, including blueberry, nougat, yogurt, and biscuit. In winter the pavement terrace is heated. *Lugeck 7.* ☎ *01 512 7979. AE, DC, MC, V. Daily 7.30am–midnight. U-Bahn 1/3 (Stephansplatz).*

★ Zu Ebener Erde und Erste Stock SPITTELBERG BOHEMIAN

Expect a cozy Biedermeier atmosphere at this family-run café, as you tuck into hearty gulasch and similar Austro-Hungarian dishes. *Burgstrasse 13.* ☎ *01 523 6254. Entrees €6.90–€12.90. AE, V. Breakfast, lunch & dinner Mon–Fri. U-Bahn 2/3 (Volkstheater).*

★★★ kids Zu den 2 Lieserl'n

NEUBAU VIENNESE The pea-green façade hides a well-kept secret: This little-known rustic restaurant with a courtyard garden serves some of the finest (and largest) schnitzels in Vienna. *Burggasse 63.* ☎ *01 523 3282. Entrees €7–€11.90. No credit cards. Daily 11am–11pm. U-Bahn 2/3 (Volkstheater).*

Zwölf Apostelkeller—fine wines, Heurige music and a rustic beer-hall atmosphere.

★★★ Zu den 3 Buchteln MAR-
GARETEN BOHEMIAN/RUSSIAN
Come to this tiny, old-world restaurant for delicious Bohemian and Russian country-style fare, Czech beers, and tasty hot desserts, served in a homely atmosphere. *Wehrgasse 9.* ☎ *01 587 8365. Entrees €8.40–€13.75. V only. Dinner Mon–Sat. U-Bahn 4 (Pilgramgasse).*

★ Zum Basilisken CITY CENTER
VIENNESE   A pretty rustic inn at the heart of the old city center, serving *Altwiener Küche* (Old-Viennese cuisine), with specialty seasonal game dishes. *Schönlaterngasse 3–5.* ☎ *01 513 3123. Entrees €10.50–€17.50. AE, DC, MC, V. Lunch & dinner daily. U-Bahn 1/4 (Schwedenplatz).*

★★ Zum Roten Elefanten MQ
AUSTRIAN   The 'Red Elephant' has become part of Vienna's in-scene, with a daily-changing menu of straightforward seasonal dishes. The set lunch menu (€7.50 for two courses) is excellent value; dinner is à la carte. *Gumpendorferstrasse 3.* ☎ *01 966 8008. Entrees €12.50–€17. No credit cards. Lunch and dinner Mon–Fri, dinner Sat. U-Bahn 2 (Museumsquartier).*

★ Zur Goldenen Glocke MAR-
GARETEN VIENNESE   Entering this ancient tavern is like arriving in the countryside. Gingham-checked tablecloths and hunting scenes decorate the interior. The menu features authentic Viennese cuisine. *Kettenbrückengasse 9.* ☎ *01 587 5767. Entrees €8.80–€14.80. DC, MC, V. Mon–Sat 11am–2.30pm, 5.30pm–midnight, Sun 11.30–3pm. U-Bahn 4 (Kettenbrückengasse).*

★★★ Zwölf Apostelkeller CITY
CENTER HEURIGE   There's always a jolly atmosphere at this medieval, vaulted *Heurige* in the heart of the old town. It offers superb wines, a lengthy menu of Austrian dishes, and live music every night. *Sonnenfelsgasse 3.* ☎ *01 512 6777. AE, DC, MC, V. Lunch & dinner daily. U-Bahn 1/3 (Stephansplatz).* ●

Nightlife Best Bets

Best for Party Animals
★★★ Passage, *Babenburgerpassage, Burgring 1 (p 130)*

Best Jazz Club
★★ Jazzland, *Franz-Josefs-Kai 29 (p 131)*

Best Bar to Wear a Bikini
★★★ Badeschiff, *Donaukanallände (p 130)*

Best for Celebrity-Spotting
★★★ Eden Bar, *Liliengasse 2 (p 131)*

Best Beer
★★★ Siebenstern Bräuwirtshaus, *Siebensterngasse 19 (p 130)*

Best for 'Chilling'
★★★ Icebar Vienna, *U-Bahnbögen 186-188, Döblinger Gürtel (p 132)*

Best Wines
★★★ Meinl's Weinbar, *Näglergasse 8 (p 129)*

Best Dance Club
★★★ Flex, *Donaukanal (by the Augartenbrücke) (p 130)*

Best Cocktail Lounge
★★ Planter's Club, *Zelinkagasse 4 (p 131)*

Best Canalside Venue
★★★ Summer Stage, *Rossauer Lände (p 73)*

Best Dressed Crowd
★★★ Red Room, *Stubenring 20 (p 129)*

Best for Romance
★★★ Aux Gazelles, *Rahlgasse 5 (p 129)*

Best People Watching
★★★ Volksgarten, *Burgring 1 (p 131)*

Best for Cutting-Edge Sounds
★★ rhiz, *Stadtbahnbögen 37-38, Lerchenfelder Gürtel (p 132)*

Most Eccentric Bar
★★★ phil, *Gumpendorfer Strasse 10-12 (p 129)*

Best Country-Style Bar
★★ Landsknecht-Treff, *Naschmarkt 217-219 (p 129)*

Best Views
★★ Onyx, *Stephansplatz 12 (p 13)*

Best Jugendstil Bar
★★ American Bar, *Kärntner Durchgang 10 (p 35)*

Best Beach Party in the City
★★ Strandbar Herrmann, *Herrmannpark/Urania (p 130)*

Most Eccentric Bar: Phil's.

Nightlife Neubau & Naschmarkt

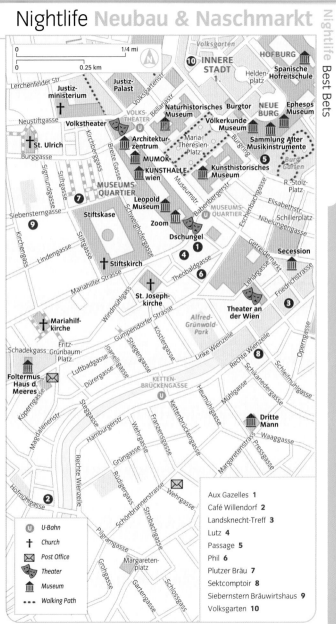

Aux Gazelles **1**
Café Willendorf **2**
Landsknecht-Treff **3**
Lutz **4**
Passage **5**
Phil **6**
Plutzer Bräu **7**
Sektcomptoir **8**
Siebernstern Bräuwirtshaus **9**
Volksgarten **10**

Nightlife City Center

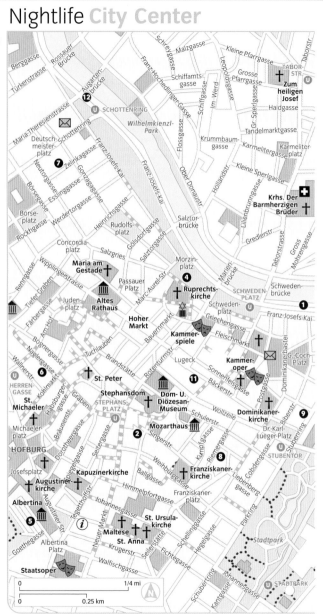

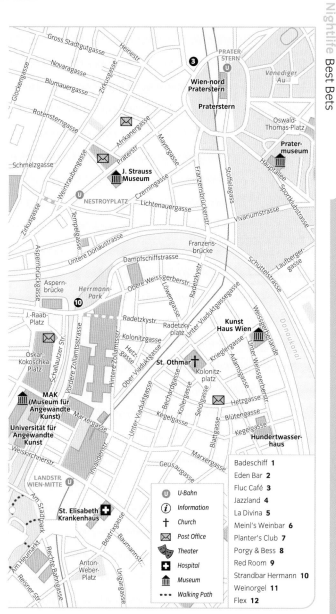

U-Bahn	
Information	
Church	
Post Office	
Theater	
Hospital	
Museum	
Walking Path	

Badeschiff 1
Eden Bar 2
Fluc Café 3
Jazzland 4
La Divina 5
Meinl's Weinbar 6
Planter's Club 7
Porgy & Bess 8
Red Room 9
Strandbar Hermann 10
Weinorgel 11
Flex 12

Nightlife **Gürtel**

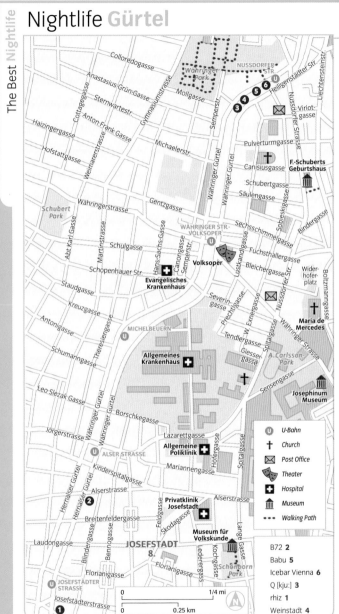

Legend:

U	U-Bahn
†	Church
✉	Post Office
🎭	Theater
✚	Hospital
🏛	Museum
•••	Walking Path

B72 **2**
Babu **5**
Icebar Vienna **6**
Q [kju:] **3**
rhiz **1**
Weinstadt **4**

Vienna Nightlife A to Z

Bars

★★★ Aux Gazelles MQ   This tiny oriental-themed club is great for chilling out to mellow Arabian rhythms. While away the evening sipping exotic cocktails Bedouin-style on comfy cushions in its intimate, sumptuous interior. *Rahlgasse 5.* ☎ *01 585 6645. www.auxgazelles.at. €10 cover. U-Bahn 2 (Museums-quartier). Map p 125.*

★ La Divina CITY CENTER Founded in homage to the operatic heroine, Maria Callas, this unique champagne bar relays live opera transmissions (minus the sound-track) from the nearby Staatsoper. It's a popular place for pre- or post-performance drinks. *Hanuschgasse 3.* ☎ *01 513 4319. www.ladivina.at. Tram 1/2/D/J (Oper). Map p 126.*

★★ Landsknecht-Treff NASCHMARKT   Stepping into this small, rustic bar in the heart of the Naschmarkt is like walking into a cosy Austrian country pub. Pine-clad, warm and homely, you're sure to receive a warm welcome, excellent local wines or beers and, if you're lucky, some snacks fresh from the market. *Naschmarkt 217-219.* ☎ *0676 723 8880. U-Bahn 1/2/4 (Karlsplatz). Map p 125.*

★★ Lutz MQ   A lively crowd frequents the trendy Lutz bar with its gleaming cocktail bar, wraparound leather banquettes, and cigar menu. There's a choice of over 200 cocktails, long drinks, and champagnes. Arrive after 10pm. *Mariahilfer-strasse 3.* ☎ *01 585 3646. www.lutz-bar.at. U-Bahn 2 (Museumsquartier). Map p 125.*

★★★ Meinl's Weinbar CITY CEN-TER   Informal yet classy, this beautiful basement wine-bar is part of the

This tiny city-centre wine bar is an atmospheric venue for some wine-tasting.

city's celebrated Meinl delicatessen empire. It serves an impressive menu of wines, grappas, champagnes, and brandies by the glass. *Näglergasse 8.* ☎ *01 532 33 34 6100. U-Bahn 1/3 (Stephansplatz). Map p 126.*

★★★ phil MQ   A quirky bar/funky furniture shop resembling a large sitting-room, except that everything has a price tag attached. Join the laid-back (non-smoking) crowd, and browse through the books and vinyl records. *Gumpendorferstrasse 10–12.* ☎ *01 581 0489. www.phil. info. U-Bahn 2 (Museumsquartier). Map p 125.*

★★★ Red Room RINGSTRASSE Located beneath Comida (a smart Hispano-Caribbean restaurant), this über-chic red bar serves exemplary cocktails to the smart set while the DJ spins lively Black beats on an illuminated dance floor. *Stubenring 20.* ☎ *01 512 4024. www.comida.at/redroom. U-Bahn 3 (Stubentor). Map p 126.*

★★ **Sektcomptoir** NASCHMARKT Just off the Naschmarkt, this diminutive locals' bar is an ideal place to relax and relish a glass of *Sekt* (sparkling wine) after a long day's sightseeing. *Schleifmühlgasse 19.* ☎ *0664 432 5388. www.sektcomptoir.at. U-Bahn 1/2/4 (Karlsplatz).*

★★ **Strandbar Herrmann** CITY CENTER   Soak up the holiday mood at this lively summertime beach bar beside the Danube Canal, with its golden sandy beach, Mediterranean-style bar, cheerful cocktails, and trendy DJ sounds. *Herrmannpark/Urania.* ☎ *No phone. www.strandbarherrmann.at. U-Bahn 1/4 (Schwedenplatz). Map p 126.*

★★★ **Weinorgel** CITY CENTER   A tiny brick-clad wine-bar in the vaults of a former Gothic monastery. Peanuts and sawdust bestrew a simple wooden floor. World wines by the glass. *Bäckerstrasse 2.* ☎ *01 513 1227. www.weinorgel.at. U-Bahn 1/3 (Stephansplatz). Map p 126.*

Beer Cellars

★★ **Plutzer Bräu** SPITTELBERG This hugely popular loft-style *Bierkeller* with brick vaulting and long, blond-wood tressel tables is a Spittelberg stalwart. In summer, the tables spill on to a lovely cobbled terrace. *Schrankgasse 2.* ☎ *01 526 1215. www.plutzerbraeu.at. Tram 49 (Stiftgasse). Map p 125.*

★★★ **Siebenstern Bräuwirtshaus** NEUBAU   A lively brew-pub with its own range of eight distinctive beers brewed in situ and served in rustic cellar rooms or under the shade of chestnut trees in the beer-garden. Try the Chili Beer. *Siebensterngasse 19.* ☎ *01 523 8697. www.7stern.at. Tram 49 (Stiftgasse). Map p 125.*

Dance Clubs

★★★ **Badeschiff** CITY CENTER Enjoy cocktails and DJ sounds from hip-hop and Indie to Turbo-Folk and Balkan beats on this funky summertime moored 'ship' on the Danube Canal. There's a swimming pool too. *Donaukanal-lände (between Schwedenbrücke and Urania).* ☎ *0699 1513 0749. www. badeschiff.at. U-Bahn 1/4 (Schwedenplatz). Map p 126.*

★★★ **Flex** ALSERGRUND   The best dance club in town, famous for its awesome sound system, with top-notch DJs and a huge variety of cutting-edge beats, including techno, indie, and underground rock. Go on Tuesday nights for Viennese electronica at its best. *Donaukanal (by the Augartenbrücke).* ☎ *01 533 7525. www.flex.at. €3 cover. U-Bahn 2/4 (Schottenring). Map p 126.*

★★★ **passage** RINGSTRASSE This futuristic club in a former subway has minimalist décor and an ultra-cool lighting system. Backdrops morph to suit varying sounds (house, disco, hip-hop, funk, etc.) on different nights. *Babenburgerpassage, Burgring 1.* ☎ *01 961 8800. www.sunshine.at. Tram 1/2/D/J (Burgring). Map p 125.*

★★ **Planter's Club** ALSERGRUND The leather seats and potted palms of this colonial-style bar attract a chic set for cocktails and a wide choice of rum and whisky, plus lively Latin beats on the small dance floor. *Zelinkagasse 4.* ☎ *01 533 3393-15. www.plantersclub.com. U-Bahn 2/4 (Schottenring). Map p 126.*

★★★ Volksgarten RINGSTRASSE
Vienna's beautiful people love this hot and happening party complex. It's all here—house, hip-hop, soul, techno, funk, salsa . . . plus an idyllic garden and an electronic roof that opens for moonlit dancing in summer. *Burgring 1.* ☎ *01 485 8924. www.volksgarten.at. €5–€15 (depending on event). Tram 1/2/D/J (Burgring). Map p 125.*

Gay & Lesbian
★★ Café Willendorf
NASCHMARKT   The affectionately named Rosa Lila Villa (pink-purple villa) is at the heart of the Viennese gay and lesbian scene. There's a lovely courtyard garden in summer. *Linke Wienzeile 102.* ☎ *01 587 1789. www.cafe-willendorf.at. U-Bahn 4 (Pilgramgasse). Map p 125.*

Indie and underground rock at Flex.

Sekt (sparkling wine) is a popular aperitif in many of Vienna's bars, and especially here at the Sektcomptoir.

Live Music
★★★ Eden Bar CITY CENTER
Anyone who's anyone in Vienna drinks at this atmospheric, sophisticated bar with its plush-red, Art-Deco interior and live music nightly from 10pm. Dress smartly (men must wear ties). *Liliengasse 2.* ☎ *01 512 7450. www.edenbar.at. U-Bahn 1/3 (Stephansplatz). Map p 126.*

★ Fluc Café PRATER   This
rugged bar is one of the best places in town to hear live, experimental, electronic, and indie acts, while Fluc Wanne in the basement stages electro and disco parties putting on a broad range of DJ sounds. *Praterstern 5.* ☎ *No phone. www.fluc.at. U-Bahn 1/2 (Praterstern). Map p 126.*

★★ Jazzland CITY CENTER   For
over 30 years, this brick-built club in a cellar under Ruprechtskirche (St. Rupert's Church) has showcased the best of Austrian and international

jazz, from blues, Dixie, and swing to modern jazz. *Franz-Josefs-Kai 29.* ☎ *01 533 2575. www.jazzland.at. U-Bahn 1/4 (Schwedenplatz). Map p 126.*

★★ Porgy & Bess STADTPARK

This relaxed, modern jazz joint in a former porn cinema is hugely popular thanks to its eclectic program of world-class, home-grown and international modern and non-traditional jazz acts. *Riemergasse 11.* ☎ *01 512 8811. www.porgy.at. U-Bahn 3 (Stubentor). Map p 126.*

Gürtel Party Tour

The *Gürtel* ring-road is currently the nerve center of Vienna's nightlife. Beneath the Jugendstil arches of the city railway designed by Otto Wagner lies a mixed bag of dance clubs, pubs, and bars. It's the in-place to party all night long to the sound of trains rumbling overhead. Start: Josefstädter Strasse U-Bahn station.

★★ rhiz

One of the cradles of Vienna's renowned electronica scene, this laid-back Internet café-bar remains a popular platform for new projects and experiments in electronic music. *Stadtbahnbögen 37-38, Lerchenfelder Gürtel.* ☎ *01 409 2505. www.rhiz.org. Map p 128.*

★ B72

Situated under Arch 72 of the Gürtel (ring-road), this old-timer's specialty is alternative live music and electronic sounds. Dark, smoky, and split-level, it draws a lively young crowd. *Stadtbahnbögen 72, Hernalser Gürtel.* ☎ *01 409 2128. www.b72.at. Map p 128.*

★★★ Q [kju:]

There's always a great party mood at Q, where the clientele are young and carefree, the cocktails potent, the barmen flashy and the dance music loud. It's easy to find, occupying three arches bathed in pink, red, and green fluorescent light. Relaxed door policy. *Stadtbahnbögen 142-144, Währinger Gürtel.* ☎ *No phone. www.kju-bar.at. Map p 128.*

★★ Weinstadt

This soothing wine-bar, simply decorated with bare brick vaults, is the perfect place to relax with friends. It offers an excellent choice of local and international wines, including chalkboard specials, to wash down platters of cold cuts, cheeses, and olives. *Stadtbahnbögen 154, Währinger Gürtel.* ☎ *01 319 6538. www.weinstadt.cc. Map p 128.*

★★★ Babu

The place to see and be seen, this long-standing cocktail lounge and dance club attracts a cool crowd. It's a lively venue on several floors. Dress smartly, there's a strict door policy. *Stadtbahnbögen 181-184, Nussdorferstasse.* ☎ *01 479 4849. www.babu.at. Cover charge varies. Map p 128.*

★★★ Icebar Vienna

Chill out literally here. Everything is made of ice: the bar, the seats, even the glasses. Never mind the temperature (minus 5°). You get suitable clothing when you arrive. *Stadtbahnbögen 186-188, Döblinger Gürtel.* ☎ *01 367 0216. www.icebarvienna.com. €18 cover charge (includes first cocktail). Map p 128.* ●

Arts & Entertainment Best Bets

Best **Acoustics**
★★★ Musikverein,
*Karlsplatz/Bösendorferstrasse 12
(p 137)*

Most **Angelic Choirboys**
★★★ Wiener Sängerknaben,
Schweizerhof (p 137)

Best **Show for Kids**
★★ Lilarum Puppet Theater, *Göllnergasse 8 (p 139)*

Best **"Jungle" in Town**
★★ Dschungel Wien, *Museumsplatz 1 (p 139)*

Most **Palatial Setting for a
Concert**
★ Schönbrunner Schlosskonzerte,
Orangerie Schönbrunn (p 137)

The **Hottest Ticket in Town**
★★★ Staatsoper, *Opernring 2
(p 139)*

Best **Ecclesiastical Sounds**
★★ Augustinerkirche, *Augustinerstrasse 3 (p 137)*

Best **Cinema to Snooze in**
★★★ Burgkino, *Opernring 19
(p 138)*

Best **Place to Meet a Mozart
Look-alike**
Konzerte im Mozarthaus, *Singer-
strasse 7 (p 137)*

Best **Chance of Getting Stand-
ing-Room Tickets**
★★ Volksoper, *Währingerstrasse 78
(p 139)*

Best **Ballet**
★★★ Das Ballett der Wiener
Staatsoper und Volksoper, *Opern-
ring 2 (p 138)*

Best acoustics at Musikverein.

Arts & Entertainment **City Center**

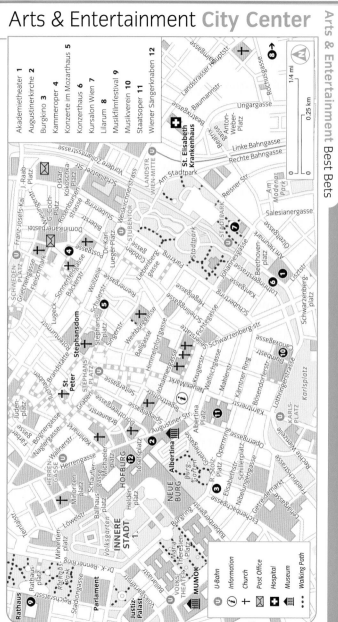

Akademietheater **1**
Augustinerkirche **2**
Burgkino **3**
Kammeroper **4**
Konzerte im Mozarthaus **5**
Konzerthaus **6**
Kursalon Wien **7**
Lilarum **8**
Musikfilmfestival **9**
Musikverein **10**
Staatsoper **11**
Wiener Sängerknaben **12**

U-Bahn
Information
Church
Post Office
Hospital
Museum
Walking Path

A & E MQ

Dschungel Wien **1**
Raimund Theater **2**
Schönbrunner
Schlosskonzerte **3**
Tanzquartier Wien **4**
Theater an der Wien **5**
Volkstheater **6**

U U-Bahn
† Church
🏛 Museum
• • • Walking Path

A & E City Center West

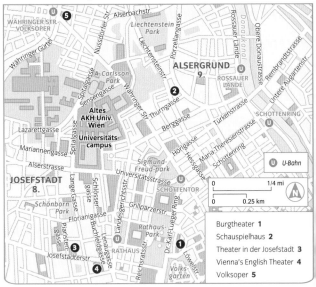

Burgtheater **1**
Schauspielhaus **2**
Theater in der Josefstadt **3**
Vienna's English Theater **4**
Volksoper **5**

U U-Bahn

Arts & Entertainment A to Z

Classical Music

★★ **Augustinerkirche** HOFBURG The Gothic Augustinian Church boasts fine acoustics, and sacred works by Haydn, Mozart, and Schubert are frequently performed here during Sunday Mass (11am). *Augustinerstrasse 3 (entrance on Josefsplatz).* 📞 *No phone. www. hochamt.at. Free admission. U-Bahn 3 (Herrengasse). Map p 135.*

★★ **Konzerthaus** STADTPARK A major venue for classical symphony and chamber music, played by the resident Vienna Symphony Orchestra and other renowned ensembles. *Lothringerstrasse 20.* 📞 *01 242 002. www. konzerthaus.at. Tickets (Prices vary). U-Bahn 4 (Stadtpark). Map p 135.*

★ **Konzerte im Mozarthaus** CITY CENTER Listen to Mozart, Haydn, Schubert, and Beethoven chamber music in the intimate Sala Terrena of the Deutschordenshaus, where Mozart used to live and play in 1781. Concerts Thurs–Sun. *Singerstrasse 7.* 📞 *01 911 9077. www.mozarthaus.at. Tickets €35, €42. U-Bahn 1/3 (Stephansplatz). Map p 135.*

★ **Kursalon Wien** STADTPARK Cheerfully enjoyable (albeit very touristic) soirées of Viennese waltz classics with the Salonorchester Alt Wien. *Johannesgasse 33.* 📞 *01 512 5790. www.kursalonwien.at. Tickets €39–€90 (€66–€123 including dinner). U-Bahn 4 (Stadtpark). Map p 135.*

★★★ **Musikverein** CITY CENTER Venue for the city's celebrated New Year's Day concert, played by the resident Vienna Philharmonic Orchestra, one of the finest in the world. *Karlsplatz/Bösendorferstrasse 12.* 📞 *01 505 8190. www.musikverein.at. Tickets €4 (standing only)–€85. U-Bahn 1/2/4 (Karlsplatz). Map p 135.*

★ **Schönbrunner Schlosskonzerte** SCHÖNBRUNN Step back in time at one of the daily concerts of popular Viennese classics staged in the Orangery of the Schönbrunn Palace, where Mozart once performed. *Orangerie Schönbrunn.* 📞 *01 812 5004-0. www.image vienna.com. Tickets: €39–€75. U-Bahn 4 (Schönbrunn). Map p 136.*

★★★ **Wiener Sängerknaben** HOFBURG Founded over 500 years ago, the Vienna Boys' Choir is perhaps the most famous of its kind in the world. Hear them sing Mass at the Hofburg's ancient Burgkapelle on Sundays (mid-Sept–June) at 9.15am. *Schweizerhof.* 📞 *01 553 9927. www.hofburgkapelle.at*

The Kursalon—the place to hear Strauss waltzes.

How to Get Tickets

Get details of what's on when from tourist offices, or in the listings magazine Falter (www.falter.at), published every Wednesday and available from a Tabak (newsagent) or a sidewalk kiosk. Tickets can be bought in advance directly from the individual venues or online at ticketing agencies such as Austria Ticket Online (www.austriaticket.at) or Club Ticket (www.clubticket.at).

The Wien-Ticket Pavillon ticket-booth beside the opera-house (Karajanplatz. ☎ 01 58885. Mon–Sat 10am–7pm) sells tickets for all venues. The Bundestheaterkassen (State Ticket Office) sells tickets for the Akademietheater, Burgtheater, Staatsoper, and Volksoper (Hanuschgasse 3. ☎ 01 514 447 880. www.bundestheater.at. Mon–Fri 8am–6pm, Sat–Sun 9am–noon. U-Bahn 1/2/4 Karlsplatz).

Book as early as you can: ticket sales at many venues (including the Staatsoper, Volksoper, Theater an der Wien, and Musikverein) begin one month ahead of the performance. Some venues offer limited numbers of last-minute standing-only tickets. The Staatsoper, for instance, releases 567 of these standing room tickets just 80 minutes before the performance starts—a bargain if you're patient enough to queue.

---

www.wsk.at. Tickets €5–€32. U-Bahn 3 (Herrengasse).

Dance
★★★ Das Ballett der Wiener Staatsoper und Volksoper CITY CENTER
World-class ballet productions by the *crème-de-la-crème* of these two recently merged companies—plus a glittering list of guest artistes. *Opernring 2. ☎ 01 51444–0. Tickets €2 (standing only), €7–€254. Tram 1/2/D/J (Oper). Maps p 135 & 136.*

★★★ Tanzquartier Wien MQ
Vienna's leading dance center hosts an ambitious program of local and international troupes, with the main emphasis on experimental dance. *Halle G, Kunsthalle, MuseumsQuartier, Museumsplatz 1. ☎ 01 581 3591. www.tqw.at. U-Bahn 2/3 (Volkstheater). Map p 136.*

Cinema
★★★ Burgkino RINGSTRASSE
This tiny, old-fashioned cinema shows only English-language movies, and regular late-night screenings of *The Third Man* (set in post–World War II Vienna) in its original British version. *Opernring 19. ☎ 01 587 8406. www.burgkino.at. Tickets €6–€8. Tram 1/2/D/J (Oper). Map p 135.*

★★ Muskfilmfestival
RINGSTRASSE Vienna has 15 different venues for open-air cinema during the summer festival season. Most popular is the Muskifilmfestival in Rathausplatz. When darkness falls, free screenings of opera and concerts are shown against a dramatic illuminated backdrop of the City Hall (Jun–Aug). *Rathausplatz. ☎ No phone. U-Bahn 2 (Rathaus). Map p 135.*

Opera & Musicals
★★ Kammeroper CITY CENTER
This small opera-house puts on a varied repertoire of everything from classic operetta and *opera buffa* (comic opera) to rock opera and more

Book in advance for a night at the Opera.

quirky contemporary musical theater. *Fleischmarkt 24.* 📞 *01 512 0100–77. www.wienerkammeroper.at. Tickets €5 (standing only), €15–€65. U-Bahn 1/4 (Schwedenplatz). Map p 135.*

★★ Raimund Theater MARIAHILF In recent years, this theater has made its name as the definitive venue for musical comedy, premiering the German-language versions of blockbuster hits such as *Cats* and *Phantom of the Opera*. *Wallgasse 18–20.* 📞 *01 599 77–0. www.musicalvienna. at. Tickets €10–€98. U-Bahn 6 (Gumpendorfer Strasse). Map p 136.*

★★★ Staatsoper CITY CENTER One of Europe's finest opera-houses, with daily performances from September to June and kids' opera in summer. *Opernring 2.* 📞 *01 514 442 250 (information);* 📞 *01 513 1513 (tickets). www.wiener-staatsoper.at. Tickets €2 (standing only), €7–€254. Tram 1/2/D/J (Oper). Map p 135.*

★★ Theater an der Wien NASCHMARKT   Founded in 1801 as an opera-house, this plush theater premiered Mozart's *Die Zauberflöte*, Beethoven's *Fidelio*, and Johann Strauss's *Die Fledermaus*. Today it hosts opera and musical theater. *Linke Weinzeile 6.* 📞 *01 58885. www. theater-wien.at. Tickets €11–€140. U-Bahn 1/2/ 4 (Karlsplatz). Map p 135.*

★★ Volksoper ALSERGRUND Affordable and fun, the 'People's Opera' is the city's leading

operetta-house. It also stages light opera, classical musicals, and ballet. *Währingerstrasse 78.* 📞 *01 514 44–3318. www.volksoper.at. Tickets €1.50/€2 (standing only), €4–€75. U-Bahn 6 (Volksoper). Map p 136.*

Theater
★ Akademietheater STADTPARK This excellent repertory theater (a second venue for the Burgtheater) covers everything from classic to contemporary drama. *Lisztstrasse 1.* 📞 *01 514 44–4740. www.akademie theater.at. Tickets €1.50 (standing only), €4–€48. U-Bahn 1/4 (Stadtpark). Map p 135.*

★★★ Burgtheater RINGSTRASSE The National Theatre is one of the best German-speaking theaters in the world. The resplendent foyer has stairway frescoes painted by Klimt. *Dr-Karl-Lueger-Ring 2.* 📞 *01 514 44–4440. www.burgtheater.at. Tickets €1.50 (standing only), €4–€48. Tram D/1/2 (Dr-Karl-Lueger-Ring). Map p 135.*

★★ kids Dschungel Wien MQ Language is no barrier for kids at the lively 'Jungle' family arts center with theater, dance, puppet shows, video, and music workshops for kids aged 2 and over. *Museumsplatz 1.* 📞 *01 522 0720–20. www.dschungel wien.at. Tickets €7.50. U-Bahn 2 (Museumsquartier). See p 136.*

★★ kids Lilarum Puppet Theater LANDSTRASSE   Kids (aged 3–10) find the Lilarum's mini-plays enchanting, with their charming hand- and rod-puppets. The stories seem to transcend any language barriers. *Göllnergasse 8.* 📞 *01 710 2666. www. lilarum.at. Tickets €7.60. U-Bahn 3 (Kardinal-Nagl-Platz). Map p 135.*

★★★ Schauspielhaus ALSERGRUND   Of Vienna's 50-plus theaters, the Schauspielhaus is at the forefront of contemporary productions—often of a thought-provoking, controversial, or alternative

Vienna Boys' Choir

The Vienna Boys' Choir (Wiener Sängerknaben, www.wsk.at) was founded in 1498 as part of the imperial choir. Originally it had just 12 boys. Over the centuries it grew in size, and counted musical luminaries such as Haydn and Schubert among its members. Nowadays Vienna's leading choir is a highly commercialized and rather overhyped organization. Four separate choirs, each consisting of 24 angelic choirboys, continuously tour the world, no longer dressed in imperial costumes, but in twee blue sailor-suits. In Vienna, they sing Sunday Mass in the Burgkapelle and give occasional concerts in the Musikverein.

nature. *Porzellangasse 19.* ☎ *01 317 0101-11. www.schauspielhaus.at. Tickets €18 adults; €9 students; €12 concessions. Tram D (Bauernfeldplatz). Map p 136.*

★ Theater in der Josefstadt

JOSEFSTADT   One of Vienna's oldest, best-loved, and most ornate theaters, founded in 1788, and known for its lightweight plays, comedies, and farces. *Josefstädterstrasse 24-26.* ☎ *01 42700-300. www.josefstadt.org. Tickets €5–€63. Bus 13A (Theater in der Josefstadt). Map p 136.*

★★ Vienna's English Theater

JOSEFSTADT   Continental Europe's oldest English-language theater was founded in 1963, and offers year-round showings of English and American classics, comedies, and contemporary works. *Josefgasse 12.* ☎ *01 402 1260. www.english theatre.at. Tickets €19.50–€38. U-Bahn 2 (Rathaus). Map p 136.*

★ Volkstheater

MQ   With an auditorium holding nearly a thousand, this is one of the city's largest theaters. It puts on an exceptionally broad repertoire, embracing classic and modern plays and operetta. *Neustiftgasse 1.* ☎ *01 52 111–400. www.volkstheater. at. Tickets €8–€40. U-Bahn 2/3 (Volkstheater). Map p 136.* ●

Head upstairs at the Volkstheater to the swanky chandelier-lit Rote Bar.

Lodging Best Bets

Best **Urban Luxury**
★★★ Do & Co $$–$$$$
Stephansplatz 12 (p 149)

Best **Cosy Bed & Breakfast**
★★★ The Rooms $ *Schlenther-
gasse 17 (p 154)*

Best **'Beach' Hotel**
★★ Strand Hotel Alte Donau $
Wagramerstrasse 51 (p 153)

Best **Boutique Hotel**
★★★ Altstadt $$ *Kirchengasse 41
(p 148)*

Best for **a Romantic Getaway**
★★★ Hollmann Beletage $$ *Köll-
nerhofgasse 6 (p 150)*

Best **Spa Hotel**
★★ The Ring $$$$ *Kärtner Ring 8
(p 154)*

Best **See-and-be-Seen Hotel**
★★★ Le Méridien $$–$$$$ *Opernring 13 (p 151)*

Best for **Families**
★★ Lassalle $$–$$$ *Engerthstrasse
173-5 (p 151)*

Most **Historic Hotel (also best
for chocolate cake)**
★★★ Sacher $$$$ *Philharmonikerstrasse 4 (p 153)*

Worst for **the Wallet**
★★★ Palais Coburg Residenz $$$$
Coburgbastei 4 (p 152)

Best for **Design Buffs**
★★★ Das Triest $$ *Wiedner Haupt-
strasse 12 (p 148)*

Best for **Design Buffs on a
Tight Budget**
★★ **kids** Roomz $ *Paragonstrasse 1
(p 152)*

Sacher—Vienna's most historic hotel.

Most **Eccentric Decor**
★★ Kuchlmasterei $$ *Obere Weissgerberstrasse 6 (p 151)*

Most **Humble Abode**
★★ Benediktushaus $ *Freyung 6a
(p 148)*

Most **Environmentally-Friendly
Hotel**
★★ Hotel am Stephansplatz
$$–$$$ *Stephansplatz 9 (p 150)*

Most **Spectacular Cityscapes**
★★★ Schloss Wilhelminenberg
$$–$$$ *Savoyenstrasse 2 (p 153)*

Best for **Wine Connoisseurs**
★★★ Rathaus Wein & Design $$
Lange Gasse 13 (p 152)

Most **Royal Welcome**
★★★ Imperial $$$$ *Kärtner Ring
16 (p 150)*

Lodging **City Center South**

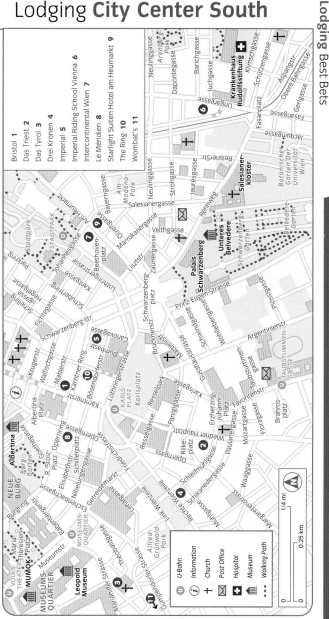

Bristol **1**
Das Triest **2**
Das Tyrol **3**
Drei Kronen **4**
Imperial **5**
Imperial Riding School Vienna **6**
Intercontinental Wien **7**
Le Méridien **8**
Starlight Suiten Hotel am Heumarkt **9**
The Ring **10**
Wombat's **11**

Legend:
- U-Bahn
- (i) Information
- + Church
- ⊠ Post Office
- ✚ Hospital
- 🏛 Museum
- ··· Walking Path

0 — 1/4 mi
0 — 0.25 km

Lodging **City Center**

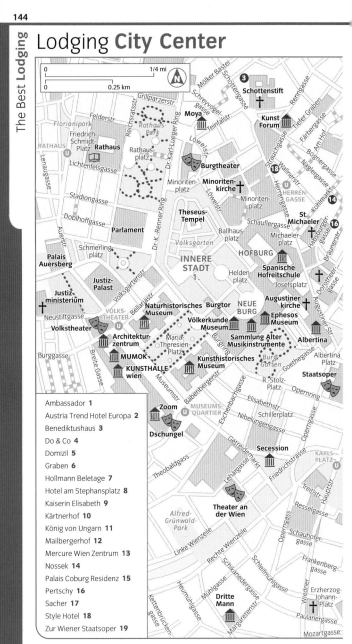

Ambassador **1**
Austria Trend Hotel Europa **2**
Benediktushaus **3**
Do & Co **4**
Domizil **5**
Graben **6**
Hollmann Beletage **7**
Hotel am Stephansplatz **8**
Kaiserin Elisabeth **9**
Kärtnerhof **10**
König von Ungarn **11**
Mailbergerhof **12**
Mercure Wien Zentrum **13**
Nossek **14**
Palais Coburg Residenz **15**
Pertschy **16**
Sacher **17**
Style Hotel **18**
Zur Wiener Staatsoper **19**

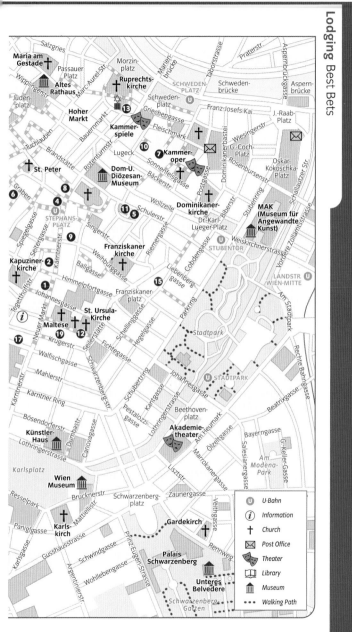

Lodging **City Center West**

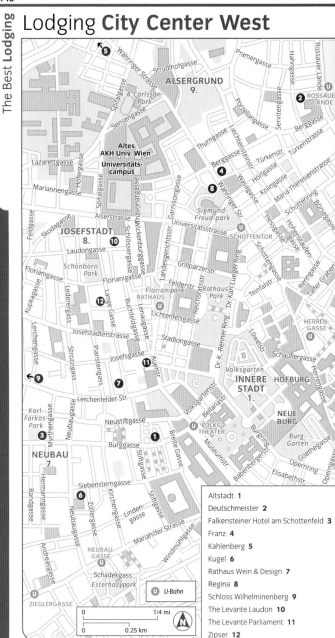

Altstadt **1**

Deutschmeister **2**

Falkensteiner Hotel am Schottenfeld **3**

Franz **4**

Kahlenberg **5**

Kugel **6**

Rathaus Wein & Design **7**

Regina **8**

Schloss Wilhelminenberg **9**

The Levante Laudon **10**

The Levante Parliament **11**

Zipser **12**

U U-Bahn

0   1/4 mi

0   0.25 km

Lodging **Danube**

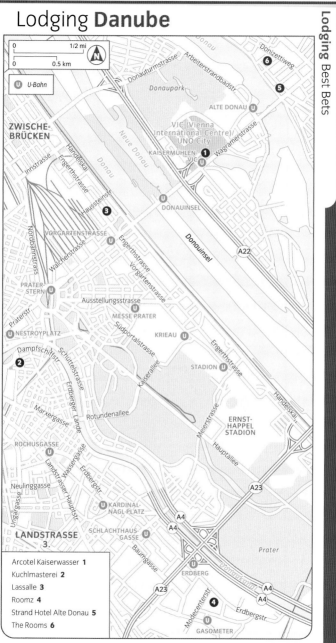

Arcotel Kaiserwasser **1**
Kuchlmasterei **2**
Lassalle **3**
Roomz **4**
Strand Hotel Alte Donau **5**
The Rooms **6**

Vienna Lodging **A to Z**

★★★ **Altstadt** SPITTELBERG
Exotic and decadent yet homely, this boutique hotel in a converted patrician house oozes style, with lavish wallpapers, velvets, and free-standing baths. *Kirchengasse 41.* ☎ *01 522 6666. www.altstadt.at. 42 units. Doubles €129–€189 w/break-fast. AE, DC, MC, V. U-Bahn 2/3 (Volks-stheater).*

★ **Ambassador** CITYCENTER
Add your name to the visitors' book alongside such luminaries as com-poser Franz Lehár, actress Marlene Dietrich, and writer Mark Twain at this upscale hotel. *Kärntnerstrasse 22/Neuer Markt 5.* ☎ *01 961 610. www.ambassador.at. 80 units. Dou-bles €230–€270. AE, DC, MC, V. U-Bahn 1/3 (Stephansplatz).*

★★ kids **Arcotel Kaiserwasser**
DANUBE   A large, modern hotel next to UNO City, with its own gar-dens, wellness center and beach area, all just a 10-minute U-Bahn ride from the city center. *Wagramer Strasse 8.* ☎ *01 224 24-0. www. arcotel.at. 282 units. Doubles €109–€650. AE, DC, MC, V. U-Bahn 1 (Kaisermühlen).*

★★ **Austria Trend Hotel Europa** CITY CENTER   Ideally located on a pedestrian street in the city center, this business-class hotel combines modern furnishings with Austrian charm. *Kärntnerstrasse 18.* ☎ *01 51594. www.austria-trend. at/euw. 158 rooms. Doubles €340. AE, DC, MC, V. U-Bahn 1/3 (Stephansplatz).*

★★ **Benediktushaus** FREYUNG
A convenient, affordable alternative to a standard city-center hotel, this guesthouse is run by Benedictine monks, with simple rooms overlook-ing tranquil cloisters. *Freyung 6a.*

☎ *01 5349 8900. www.schottenstift. at. 21 units. Doubles €99–€107 w/breakfast. AE, DC, MC, V. U-Bahn 2 (Schottentor).*

★★ kids **Bristol** RINGSTRASSE
The exuberant marble lobby of this landmark hotel belies the tasteful *fin-de-siècle* charm of its rooms. For the ultimate indulgence, reserve the Prince of Wales suite. *Kärntner Ring 1.* ☎ *01 515 160. www.luxury collection.com/bristol. 140 units. Doubles €235–€630. AE, DC, MC, V. Tram 1/2/D/J (Oper).*

★★★ **Das Triest** MARIAHILF
Formerly used as a stable on the Vienna–Trieste stagecoach route in the 17th century, this boutique hotel now has chic modern interiors designed by Sir Terence Conran, attracting an arty clientele. *Wiedner Hauptstrasse 12.* ☎ *01 589 180. www.dastriest.at. 72 units. Doubles €265–€273 w/breakfast. AE, DC, MC, V. Tram 62/65 (Paulanergasse).*

The stylish Altstadt.

Arcotel Kaiserwasser.

★★ Das Tyrol MQ This small luxury hotel near the MuseumsQuartier offers friendly service, comfortable stylish rooms, and an impressive collection of contemporary Austrian art. *Mariahilfer Straße 15.* ☎ *01 587 5415. www.das-tyrol.at. 30 units. Doubles €149–€259 w/breakfast. AE, DC, MC, V. U-Bahn 2 (Museumsquartier).*

★ Deutschmeister SERVITEN Just a few minutes' walk from the Ringstrasse, this friendly hotel offers good value, with clean, simple rooms and a superb buffet breakfast. *Grünentorgasse 30.* ☎ *01 310 3404. www.city-hotels.at. 52 units. Doubles €98–€240 w/breakfast. AE, DC, MC, V. U-Bahn 4 (Rossauer Lände).*

★★★ Do & Co CITY CENTER Sophisticated suede walls, teak floors and deep sofas are the hallmarks of this glossy, bulbous hotel and rooftop restaurant in the iconic Haas Haus, with unparalleled views over Stephansplatz and the cathedral. *Stephansplatz 12.* ☎ *01 24188. www.doco.com. 43 units. Doubles €220–€450. AE, DC, MC, V. U-Bahn 1/3 (Stephansplatz).*

★★ Domizil CITYCENTER This charming hotel has light, spacious rooms and a homely atmosphere. It is ideally placed for shopping and sightseeing in the city center. *Schulerstrasse 14.* ☎ *01 513 3199. www.hoteldomizil.at. 40 units.* *Doubles €125–€185 w/breakfast. AE, DC, MC, V. U-Bahn 1/3 (Stephansplatz).*

★★ Drei Kronen NASCHMARKT The 'Three Crowns' (of Austria, Hungary and Bohemia) are carved on the façade of this simple but comfortable hotel. Ask for a room overlooking the Naschmarkt. *Schliefmühlgasse 25.* ☎ *01 587 3289. www.hotel3kronen.at. 41 units. Doubles €70–€115 w/breakfast. AE, DC, MC, V. U-Bahn 1/2/4 (Karlsplatz).*

★★ Falkensteiner Hotel am Schottenfeld NEUBAU Dramatic colored-lighting effects distinguish this trendy, modern hotel. It attracts a young and savvy clientele. *Schottenfeldgasse 74.* ☎ *01 526 5181. www.falkensteiner.com/schottenfeld. 95 units. Doubles €129–€219 w/breakfast. AE, DC, MC, V. Tram 48 (Zieglergasse/Burggasse).*

★★ Franz SCHOTTENRING Furnished in Old-Viennese baroque style, this cozy pension is a popular budget choice. Its interconnected rooms are well suited to family groups. *Währingerstrasse 12.* ☎ *01 310 4040-0. www.hotelpensionfranz. at. 24 units. €89–€95 w/breakfast. AE, DC, MC, V. U-Bahn 2 (Schottentor).*

★★ Graben CITYCENTER Smart and central, there's no better location

Boutique Hotel Das Triest.

if you want to hit the main shopping streets. Ask for a superior double room. *Dorotheergasse 3.* ☎ *01 512 1531. www.kremslehnerhotels.at. 41 units. Doubles €180–€255 w/breakfast. AE, DC, MC, V. U-Bahn 1/3 (Stephansplatz).*

★★★ Hollmann Beletage CITY CENTER Spacious rooms, designer furniture, and plenty of home comforts make this inner-city sanctuary a welcoming bolt hole. *Köllnerhofgasse 6.* ☎ *01 961 1960. www. hollman-beletage.at. 16 rooms. Doubles €140–€180 w/breakfast. AE, DC, MC, V. U-Bahn 1/4 (Schwedenplatz).*

★★ kids Hotel am Stephansplatz CITY CENTER The central location of this hotel (right next to the cathedral) is unbeatable. Run on eco-friendly lines (sustainable wood, organic meals, recycling), its organic breakfasts are delicious. *Stephansplatz 9.* ☎ *01 53 405–0. www.hotelamstephansplatz.at. 56 units. Doubles €190–€250 w/breakfast. AE, DC, MC, V. U-Bahn 1/3 (Stephansplatz).*

★★★ kids Imperial RINGSTRASSE This sumptuous hotel conjures up the glory days of the Habsburg empire with its palatial rooms. It's the pick of the bunch for visiting heads of state. *Kärtner Ring 16.* ☎ *01 501 10–0. www.luxury collection.com/imperial. 138 units.*

Doubles €355–€880. AE, DC, MC, V. Tram 1/2/D (Schwarzenbergplatz).

★ Imperial Riding School Vienna BELVEDERE This elegant neoclassical hotel near the Belvedere is set in a former riding school. It has an indoor pool, fitness center, and garden. *Ungargasse 60.* ☎ *01 711 75–0. www.imperialrenaissance.at. 360 units. Doubles €129–€159. AE, DC, MC, V. Tram O (Rennweg).*

★ Intercontinental Wien STADTPARK The stark modern façade conceals a palatial interior of lavish décor and top-notch amenities, including business and fitness centers. *Johannesgasse 28.* ☎ *01 711 22–0. www.intercontinental. com/vienna. 453 units. Doubles €180–€400. AE, DC, MC, V. U-Bahn 4 (Stadtpark).*

★★ Kärtnerhof CITYCENTER Hidden down a tiny lane, this quiet, friendly hotel has traditional furnishings and a roof terrace. It makes a popular choice for budget-conscious visitors. *Grasshofgasse 4.* ☎ *01 512 1923. www.kartnerhof.com. 44 units. Doubles €85–€167 w/breakfast. AE, DC, MC, V. U-Bahn 1/4 (Schwedenplatz).*

★★ Kahlenberg JOSEFSDORF Among the vineyards of the Vienna Woods with superb views of the metropolis, this ultra-modern hotel makes an idyllic retreat from urban life. *Josefsdorf 2.* ☎ *01 328 1500. www.austria-trend.at/kaw. 20 units. €250–€450. AE, DC, MC, V. U-Bahn 4 (Heiligenstadt) then Bus 38A (Kahlenberg).*

★★ **Kaiserin Elisabeth** CITYCENTER   Formerly frequented by Mozart, Wagner and Liszt, this hotel offers traditional Viennese elegance with sumptuous (if slightly over-the-top) furnishings. *Weihburggasse 3.* ☎ *01 515 26–0. www.kaiserin elisabeth.at. 63 units. Doubles €208–€245 w/breakfast. AE, DC, MC, V. U-Bahn 1/3 (Stephansplatz).*

★★★ **König von Ungarn** CITY CENTER   Step inside and take a time-warp trip to the days when this grand hotel served as a guesthouse for cathedral dignitaries and Mozart lived next door. *Schulerstrasse 10.* ☎ *01 515 84–0. www.kuv.at. 33 units. Doubles €215 w/breakfast. AE, DC, MC, V. U-Bahn 1/3 (Stephansplatz).*

★★ **Kuchlmasterei** PRATER   Small, stylish, and quirky, Kuchlmasterei began life as a restaurant before adding several opulent suites. Treat yourself to the special bath menu. *Obere Weissgerberstrasse 6.* ☎ *01 712 9000. www. kuchlmasterei.at. 7 units. AE, DC, MC, V. Suite €247. Tram N/O (Hintere Zollamtsstrasse).*

★★ **Kugel** SPITTALBERG   The perfect choice for an affordable romantic break in the picturesque Spittalberg area, not far from the Museums-Quartier. Ask for a room with a four-poster bed. *Siebensterngasse 43.* ☎ *01 523 3355. www.hotelkugel.at. 34 units. Doubles €80–€120 w/breakfast. No credit cards. Tram 49 (Neubaugasse).*

★★ **kids Lassalle** DANUBE   Near the Donauinsel (Danube Island) beaches and the Prater funfair, this hotel is superb for families, with a games room, toddlers' play-room, and babysitters available upon request. *Engerthstrasse 173–5.* ☎ *01 213 15–0. www.austria-trend.at/law. 140 units. AE, DC, MC, V. Doubles €150–€300 w/breakfast. U-Bahn 1 (Vorgartenstrasse).*

★★★ **Le Méridien** RINGSTRASSE   Relax in the sophisticated spa, then join the smart set for cocktails in the glamorous Shambala Bar. Bedrooms are sleekly minimalist. *Opernring 13.* ☎ *01 588 900. www.vienna.le meridien.com. 294 units. Doubles €180–€320. AE, DC, MC, V. Tram 1/2/D/J (Oper).*

★★ **Mailbergerhof** CITYCENTER   A gorgeous small hotel in a small baroque palace with stables and its own chapel, just a stone's throw from the cathedral and the opera-house. *Annagasse 7.* ☎ *01 512 0641. www. mailbergerhof.at. 40 units. Doubles*

Living room, Hollmann Beletage.

Terrace, Rathaus Wein & Design.

€180–€260 w/breakfast. AE, DC, MC, V. U-Bahn 1/3 (Stephansplatz).

★ **Mercure Wien Zentrum** CITY-CENTER   The most central of several Mercure chain hotels, well placed for exploring the lively Bermuda Triangle nightlife zone. Accommodation is predictably functional, but good value. *Fleischmarkt 1a.* ☎ *01 534 60–0. www.mercure. com. 154 units. Doubles €150–€190. AE, DC, MC, V. U-Bahn 1/4 (Schwedenplatz).*

★★ **kids Nossek** CITY CENTER   Sample true Viennese hospitality in an excellent central location at this friendly little guesthouse, furnished in baroque style. *Graben 17.* ☎ *01 533 7041–0. www.pension-nossek. at. 32 units. Doubles €115–€143 w/breakfast. No credit cards. U-Bahn 1/3 (Stephansplatz).*

★★★ **Palais Coburg Residenz** CITY CENTER   The ultimate in traditional luxury, this regal palace has a Michelin-starred restaurant, a vast wine cellar, and a rooftop pool. *Coburgbastei 4.* ☎ *01 518 180. www.palais-coburg.com. Doubles €490–€2,140. AE, DC, MC, V. U-Bahn 3 (Stubentor).*

★★ **Pertschy** CITYCENTER   Stay in this pension in a beautiful baroque palace for its pretty, well-proportioned rooms, central location,

and frequent special offers (check the website for details). *Habsburgergasse 5.* ☎ *01 534 49–0. www.pertschy.com. 50 units. Doubles €105–€167 w/breakfast. AE, DC, MC, V. U-Bahn 1/3 (Stephansplatz).*

★★★ **Rathaus Wein & Design** JOSEFSTADT   This bijou hotel features a different Austrian vintner in the design (and mini-bar) of each room, together with frequent wine-tasting evenings for its guests. *Lange Gasse 13.* ☎ *01 400 1122. www.hotel-rathaus-wien.at. 33 units. Doubles €148–€198. U-Bahn 2/3 (Volkstheater).*

★ **Regina** SCHOTTENRING   Located in a grand city palace, the main appeal of this traditional, family-run hotel is its rather faded elegance. Ask for a room overlooking the Votivkirche. *Währingerstrasse 1.* ☎ *01 402 7995. www.kremslehner hotels.at. 148 units. Doubles €150–€225 w/breakfast. AE, DC, MC, V. U-Bahn 2 (Schottentor).*

★★ **kids Roomz** SIMMERING   A 'budget design hotel' offering smart, minimalist rooms to design-savvy visitors who can't afford city-center prices. An added bonus—it's right by the funky Gasometer development. *Paragonstrasse 1.* ☎ *01 743 1777. www.roomz-vienna.com. 152 units. Doubles €63–€109. AE, DC, MC, V. U-Bahn 3 (Gasometer).*

★★★ **Sacher** RINGSTRASSE

Vienna's most famous hotel, founded in 1876, retains its palatial 19th-century style, reveling in opulent, romantic rooms and rococo furniture. Its famous *Sachertorte* is on the must-eat list of every tourist. *Philharmonikerstrasse 4.* ☎ *01 514 560. www.sacher.com. 152 units. Doubles €376–€650. AE, DC, MC, V. Tram 1/2/D (Oper).*

★★★ **Schloss Wilhelminenberg** OTTAKRING

This former castle surrounded by parkland in the western outskirts is now a contemporary-style hotel with sensational city vistas. *Savoyenstrasse 2.* ☎ *01 485 03–0. www.austria-trend. at/wiw. 87 units. Doubles €200–€300. AE, DC, V. U-Bahn 3 (Ottakring) then Bus 46B/146B (Schloss Wilhelminenberg).*

★★★ kids **Starlight Suiten Hotel am Heumarkt** STADTPARK

Light, airy apartments and cheerful service are the hallmarks of this central hotel. Ideal for families. *Am Heumarkt 15.* ☎ *01 710 7808. www. starlighthotels.com. 50 units. Doubles €183–€211 w/breakfast. AE, DC, MC, V. U-Bahn 4 (Stadtpark).*

Smart apartment at the Starlight Suiten Hotel am Heumarkt.

★★ kids **Strand Hotel Alte Donau** DANUBE

A city 'beach' hotel, with cheerful rooms, al fresco breakfasts in summer, bikes to hire, and its very own beach complete with rowing boats. *Wagramerstrasse 51.* ☎ *01 204 4040. www.strand hotel-alte-donau.at. 33 rooms. Doubles €55–€118 w/breakfast. U-Bahn 1 (Alte Donau).*

★★ **Style Hotel** CITY CENTER

Housed in a striking Art Nouveau building, this hotel oozes modern urban-chic—think dark wood and plush velvet. Bonuses include superb bathrooms, an Italian-inspired

Strand Hotel Alte Donau.

restaurant, and the popular H12 bar. *Herrengasse 12.* ☎ *01 227 800. www.stylehotel.at. 78 units. Doubles €200–€300. U-Bahn 3 (Herrengasse).*

★★ **The Levante Laudon** JOSEF-STADT This chic, minimalist apartment-hotel, within a beautiful Biedermeier house, is popular with business clientele and families for short or extended stays. *Laudongasse 8.* ☎ *01 407 1370. www.the levante.com. 39 units. Doubles €110–€165, family rooms €160–€230. Tram 5/33 (Laudongasse).*

★★★ **The Levante Parliament** RINGSTRASSE A striking turn-of-the-century designer hotel, just behind the Austrian Parliament building, with an ultra-modern interior of light natural stone, dark wood, glass, and chrome. *Auerspergstrasse 9.* ☎ *01 228 28–0. www.thelevante.com. 70 units. Doubles €170–€355 w/breakfast. U-Bahn 2 (Rathaus).*

★★ **The Ring** RINGSTRASSE Tradition meets modernity at this five-star hotel near the opera-house. Behind a beautiful 19th-century façade, the stylish but comfortable rooms, snazzy suites, and fitness

The contemporary Style Hotel.

spa ooze casual luxury. *Kärtner Ring 8.* ☎ *01 221 22–0. www.thering hotel.at. Doubles €330–€2,550. Tram 1/2/D/J (Oper).*

★★★ kids **The Rooms** DANUBE This tiny, family-run bed & breakfast near the Old Danube is the perfect retreat for a summer weekend. It has a tranquil garden, delicious home-made breakfasts, and exotically furnished rooms. *Schlenthergasse 17.* ☎ *0664 431 6830. www.therooms.at. 4 units. Doubles €65–€110 w/breakfast. U-Bahn 1 (Kagran).*

★ **Wombat's** NEUBAU Billed as the 'city hostel', this clean, lively youth hotel is in a trendy quarter near lots of shops and bars. It serves food to hungry clubbers until after midnight. *Grangasse 6.* ☎ *01 897 2336. www.wombats-hostels.com. 300 beds (mixed or female dorms, double rooms).€19–€25. MC, V. U-Bahn 3/6 (Westbahnhof).*

★ **Zipser** JOSEFSTADT Don't be put off by the plain façade of this contemporary hotel. It's a friendly place with beautiful, generously sized bedrooms—some have tranquil, tree-shaded balconies. *Lange Gasse 49.* ☎ *01 404 54–0. www. zipser.at. 47 units. Doubles €85–€145 w/breakfast. AE, DC, MC, V. U-Bahn 2 (Rathaus).*

★ **Zur Wiener Staatsoper** RINGSTRASSE In a prime location near the opera-house, this welcoming family-run hotel oozes Viennese charm. Bedrooms have high ceilings, crystal chandeliers, and floral wallpapers. *Krugerstrasse 11.* ☎ *01 513 1274. www.zurwienerstaatsoper. at. 22 units. Doubles €111–€140 w/breakfast. AE, DC, MC, V. Tram 1/2/D/J (Oper).* ●

The
Savvy Traveler

Before You Go

Government Tourist Offices

In the US: 120 West 45th Street, 9th floor, New York, NY 10036 (☎ 1 212 944 6885); 6520 Platt Avenue, # 561 West Hills, California, CA 91307-3218 (☎ 1 818 999 4030). **In Canada:** 2 Bloor Street West, # 400 Toronto, ON, M4W 3E2 (☎ 1 416 967 4867). **In the UK & Ireland:** 9-11 Richmond Buildings, London, W1D 3HF (☎ 020 7440 3830 or 0845 101 1818 (UK); 0189 093 0118 (Ireland)). **In Australia:** 1st Floor, 36 Carrington Street, Sydney NSW 2000 (☎ 02 9299 3621). Wherever you live, the best place for information is the official website of Vienna Tourism at www.vienna.info.

The Best Time to Go

The best time to visit is from May to October. May, when the lilac and chestnut trees are in bloom, marks the start of beer-garden season. Months from June to August, when the days are long and hot, are ideal for lazy afternoons in Vienna's extensive parks; for swimming and sunbathing at the city's beaches; and for river trips and watersports on the Danube. However, Vienna can get very crowded at the height of summer, especially during school vacations. September marks the start of the theater season as all the major venues launch their new programs and, in October, the new wines from the Wienerwald vineyards are toasted in the city bars and country *Heurigen*. Another popular time is Christmas, when snow has often fallen, festive decorations and lights illuminate the city, and the streets are filled with stalls selling roasted chestnuts and *Glühwein* (mulled wine). Many visitors come to shop at the Christmas markets or to enjoy the city's celebrated New

Year's Eve festivities. Whenever you choose to visit, there's always a superb choice of theater and music and over 80 museums to provide entertainment for all the family, whatever the weather.

Climate

Vienna's mild climate means that you can enjoy visiting the city year-round. As a general rule, Vienna has cold winters, hot summers, and a mild climate during spring and fall. May marks the start of balmy days, and al fresco dining (until September). Months between June and August are the hottest with temperatures ranging from 64° to 70° F (18–22° C). This is also the wettest time of year, but the rain helps to keep the city cool and pleasant. September is one of the best months for sightseeing, with crisp, sunny days, comfortable temperatures, and fewer visitors than during high summer. October too, can be very mild and pleasant, when the leaves in the city parks and vineyards start to change color. The notorious *Föhn* wind can blow at any time of year. This warm, dry Alpine wind often brings crystal-clear days (beautiful light for photographs), but it is also blamed for headaches and bad moods. November heralds the first chills of winter. January and February are the coldest months. Snow is frequent, although it rarely settles for long in the city center. It can be surprisingly cold, so remember to bring plenty of warm clothes.

Festivals & Special Events

For further information on what's on, check out the 'Events' section of the website www.vienna.info.

VIENNA'S AVERAGE DAILY TEMPERATURE & MONTHLY RAINFALL

	JAN	FEB	MAR	APR	MAY	JUNE
Temp (°F)	26	35	53	55	59	64
Temp (°C)	-3	2	12	13	15	18
Rainfall (mm)	38	41	40	50	60	72
	JULY	AUG	SEPT	OCT	NOV	DEC
Temp (°F)	68	70	62	53	42	35
Temp (°C)	20	22	17	12	6	2
Rainfall (mm)	60	62	42	40	50	42

SPRING The **Spring Marathon** takes place from the Schönbrunn Palace to the Rathaus in April. The **Frühlingsfest** (Spring Festival) of classical music runs from April to mid-May, alternating each year between the Musikverein and the Konzerthaus. The **Wiener Festwochen** (Vienna Festival) follows in May. This is Vienna's main arts festival of opera, theater, and performing arts (from mid-May to mid-June). Spring also marks the start of the **Schönbrunn Palace concert season** (Mar–Oct), the **Prater funfair** (Apr–Oct), and performances of the **Spanish Riding School** (until June).

SUMMER Highlights of this glorious season of balls and open-air entertainment include the **Mozart Opera** series, performed nightly in the Schönbrunn Park until mid-August, and the **Donauinselfest** (last weekend in June), a three-day pop festival on Danube Island. The free **Musikfilm Festival** at the Rathaus (mid-July to mid-Sept) is one of several open-air cinema venues throughout the city. The **Vinova** wine fair takes place in the Prater (2nd week June), and Vienna's gay community celebrates late June with the frivolous **Regenbogen Parade** (Rainbow Parade). On the music front, there's the **Klangbogen** music festival (July–Aug) of opera and orchestral music in some of the city's most celebrated venues, and a **Jazz Fest** (first two weeks July) at the State Opera House and Volkstheater.

FALL Fall is the cultural start of the year, when the major theaters and opera-houses reopen for the season and launch their new programs. The **Spanish Riding School** starts to perform again (Sept–June), the **trotting races** begin in the Krieau at the Prater (until June), and the **Vienna Boys Choir** sings Mass once more on Sundays (mid-Sept–June) after their summer break. On the **Lange Nacht der Museen** (1st Sat in Oct), all the museums in the city open from 6pm to 1am, and one ticket allows entry to all of them. At the end of the month, the **National Holiday** (26 Oct) is an annual holiday celebrating the withdrawal of Allied troops in 1955, following the passing of the Neutrality Act. October also sees the start of **Wien Modern** (Oct–end Nov), a modern music festival at the Konzerthaus, and the **Viennale**, Austria's leading film festival. In November, the **Schubertiade** concert series takes place at the Musikverein, and **Christkindlmärkte,** the city's much-loved Christmas markets open (mid-Nov–end Dec).

WINTER **Christmas markets** are in full swing right across the city for the month of December, at Freyung, Karlsplatz, Spittelberg, Schönbrunn, and Heilgenkreuzerhof. On December 6, St. Nicholas and his wicked companion Krampus make their annual appearance in various **St. Nicholas festivities and parades**. Christmas is marked by **Midnight**

Mass (arrive early to get a seat in the Stephansdom). **Christmas Day** and **Stefanitag** (Boxing Day) are public holidays. **New Year's Eve** is traditionally celebrated with a performance of **Die Fledermaus** at the Opera House and Volksoper (shown on large screens in Stephansplatz); **Beethoven's 9th Symphony** is performed at the Konzerthaus; and the glittering **Kaiserball** takes place at the Hofburg. The nation's largest **Silvester** (New Year's Eve) party takes place in the city center, with street entertainment, revelry, and dazzling fireworks. The famous **New Year's Day concert** is performed by the Vienna Philharmonic at the Musikverein (requests for tickets for the following year's concert must arrive in writing at the Musikverein on Jan 2, no sooner, no later). Then there's ice-skating for everyone (mid-Jan–Feb) in front of the city hall at **Vienna Ice Dream**, followed by the **Fasching** carnival season (Jan 6–Ash Wed). Fasching festivities include the Opera Ball (last Thurs before Shrove Tues), one of the grandest society events of the year, climaxing at the lavish **Heringschmaus** (Ash Wed) buffet. The **Haydn Tage** concert series (mid-Feb–1st week Mar) takes place at the Konzerthaus.

Useful Websites

- **www.vienna.info** The official website for the Vienna Tourist Board contains lots of useful information on where to stay (including a hotel booking facility); what to do (museums, galleries, sights); where to go (restaurants, theaters, nightlife) and much more.

- **www.wien.at** The city's municipal online information service, run by local government, contains maps and all sorts of useful information, with sections on business, culture, health, leisure, history, and politics.

- **www.aboutvienna.org** A fun, English-language website devoted to the city's sightseeing, culture, and cuisine.

- **www.austria.info** The Austrian National Tourist Board's website contains everything you need to know for holidaying in Austria, plus a facility for booking accommodation.

- **www.austriatoday.at** Vienna's sole English-language newspaper is only available online.

- **www.niederoesterreich.at** Information on Niederösterreich (Lower Austria), the region surrounding Vienna.

- **www.viennaairport.com** Useful for flight planning, with details of airport services and transport to and from the city center.

- **www.oebb.at** Timetables, fares, and online booking for the national rail system, the Österreichische Bundesbahnen (ÖBB).

- **www.wienerlinien.at** Schedules and routes for the city's public transport network, including bus, tram, U-Bahn and night-bus systems, plus details of all the various ticket types on offer.

- **www.ddsg-blue-danube.at** Details of sightseeing cruises and special day-trips on the waterways of the Danube.

Cellphones (Mobiles)

Austria is on the GSM 1800 (Global System for Mobiles) wireless network, which means that world phones are the only US phones that can be used in Vienna. In Europe, check with your local network provider before leaving home, and confirm that your phone is unlocked (and therefore able to receive international calls). GSM phones work with a removable plastic SIM card, encoded with your phone number and account information. You can buy a cheap pay-as-you-go cellphone at any phone store in Austria for about €50–€80. The major networks—A-1, Drei, One, and T-Mobile —all sell SIM cards with €10 worth of calls for €39. You can top this up using phone cards purchased from supermarkets and **Trafik** (a chain of tobacconists) for €20 or €40. Local cellphone numbers start with 0650, 0660, 0664, 0676, and 0699.

Car Rentals

Don't bother! Driving in Vienna is a nightmare. You're much better sticking to the city's highly efficient public transport system. Vienna is surprisingly compact and many of the main sights are all within easy walking distance. If you really want to rent a vehicle, it is usually cheaper to reserve a car before leaving home, ready for collection at the airport. Try **Avis** (☎ 01 7007 32700, www. avis.at); **Budget** (☎ 01 7007 32711, www.budget.at); **Europcar** (☎ 01 7007 32699, www.europcar.at); **Hertz** (☎ 01 7007 32661, www. hertz.at), or **Sixt** (☎ 01 7007 36517, www.e-sixt.at).

Getting **There**

By Plane

Most visitors fly into Vienna International Airport (☎ 01 7007-0. www. viennaairport.com) at Schwechat, 20km southeast of the city center, although some European charter flights make use of the cheaper Airport Letisko Bratislava (☎ +421 2 4857 3353. www.airportbratislava.sk), just 60km east of Vienna.

At Vienna International Airport, the Vienna Tourist Service desk at Baggage Reclaim (☎ 01 7007 32875, daily 8.30am–9pm) can provide general maps and pamphlets and help you find a hotel room if you haven't reserved ahead. To reach the city center, follow signs to the S-Bahn suburban train station (☎ 01 05 1717, www.oebb.at, 5.39am–00.09am) for cheap, easy connections to the city center (running every 9 and 39 minutes past the hour). It takes 24 minutes on the S7 to reach Wien Mitte central station and costs €4.40. Note that to return to the airport, you need to catch the S2 (not the S7), which runs at 22 and 55 minutes past the hour. The City Airport Train (CAT, ☎ 01 252 50, www.cityairporttrain.com, 5.38am–11.08pm, €9)

takes 16 minutes, but it is the more expensive option. Airport Express buses (☎ 01 7007 32300, 5am–midnight, €6) shuttle every 30 minutes to Schwedenplatz in the city center, where there are U-Bahn connections. Journey time is usually about 20 minutes, depending on traffic. Expect to pay around €30 for a taxi-ride to the city center. When travelling to and from the airport, be sure to request airport rates in advance.

On arrival at Airport Letisko Bratislava, a shuttle bus operates 11 times a day to Vienna's Südtiroler Platz. It takes roughly 90 minutes and costs €9. Alternatively catch bus 61 (every 10–20 minutes, 5am–11pm) to the main station, then take a direct train to Vienna's Südbahnhof (almost hourly, 6:50am–11:50pm, €10.30). From April to October you can arrive by hydrofoil along the Danube from Bratislava in 75 minutes (☎ 01 588 80, www.ddsg-blue-danube.at). Five sailings daily, from €16). Alternatively, a taxi-ride from Bratislava airport to Vienna city center takes around 45 minutes, and costs approximately €200–€300.

By Car

Austria has an excellent network of motorways but you need an *Autobahnvignette* (toll-sticker) in order to drive on them. These are available at gas stations, tobacconists and border-crossing points, and must be attached to the inside of your windscreen. A 10-day vignette costs €7.70. The main access route from the north is on the A22 Danube motorway (*Donauuferautobahn*); from the west on the A1 western motorway (*Westautobahn*); the A2 and A23 southern motorways (*Südautobahn*); and the A4 eastern motorway (*Ostautobahn*)— the route from Schwechat International Airport. The motorways converge on the Gürtel (outer ring-road). From here, follow signs to *Zentrum* (city center).

By Train

Vienna has several mainline railway stations, three of which have international connections. As a general rule, trains from the west (and some from Budapest) arrive at the Westbahnhof; trains from the south and east at the Südbahnhof; and trains from the north at Franz-Josefs-Bahnhof. Facilities at each include a travel agency, snack-bars, newsagents, and shops. If you're arriving by Eurocity train, book in advance (you have to pay a supplement if you book within 72 hours of departure). Reserve a bed if you're traveling overnight. Many of the night trains have no buffet service, so bring some drinks and snacks with you.

By Bus

International coach connections can be long and uncomfortable so I don't really recommend them. There is no central bus station, so your arrival destination will vary, depending which company you're traveling with. Wien Mitte coach station handles most of the international coach services as well as domestic routes from eastern Austria. Domestic coach routes from southern and southwestern Austria terminate at the Südbahnhof coach station. Eurolines (☎ 01 798 2900, www.eurolines.at) offer coach services throughout Europe, arriving at the bus station at the U3 U-Bahn station of Erdberg, and occasionally at Südbahnhof.

Getting **Around**

On Foot

Vienna is easy to explore on foot. Most of the major attractions lie within the Ringstrasse, and the Tourist Office has an excellent, free map to help you. Don't worry if you get lost—the graceful tower of the Stephansdom is never far from sight and always useful for orientation.

Public Transport Ticket System

Vienna's comprehensive public transport system is clean, fast, and very efficient. It comprises the U-Bahn (underground trains), S-Bahn (regional trains), trams, and buses and it's easy to use. Flat-fare tickets are valid for all modes of transport, and can be purchased at tobacconists and in U-Bahn stations from automatic machines (with instructions in English) and occasionally staffed ticket offices. Before boarding a train, you must put your ticket in the blue validating machine (*Entwerter*) in the entrances to the U-Bahn stations. On buses and trams you must immediately stamp your ticket upon boarding. Traveling without a valid ticket can result in a heavy fine. Tickets and passes include an *Einzelfahrschein* (Single Ticket, €1.70/€2.20 if purchased on trams and buses, correct change required); a *Streifenkarte* (Strip Card, €6.80, for four journeys); a *24-Stunden Wien-Karte* (24 hours unlimited travel, €5.70); a *72-Stunden Wien-Karte* (72 hours unlimited travel, €13.60); an *8-Tage-Karte* (valid for 8 days—not necessarily consecutive ones, €27.20) and a *Wochenkarte* (valid Mon–Sun only, €12.50). The Vienna Card (€18.50) also provides 72 hours of unlimited travel plus other discounts (see Passes, p 165). Kids under six travel free; kids under 15 travel free on Sundays and during the Viennese school holidays.

By U-Bahn

The U-Bahn (underground train) is the fastest way of getting about town, although admittedly it's not as scenic as the trams. There are five color-coded routes (U1—red, U2—purple, U3—orange, U4—green, U6—brown). Transport maps are posted in all stations; free maps are available from Wiener Linien (☎ 01 790 9100, www.wienerlinien.at); and an electronic board on the platform indicates the destination of the next train and the waiting time until its arrival. The U-Bahn runs daily from about 5am until just after midnight, with trains at approximately 5-minute intervals (more frequent at rush hour); every 7–8 minutes after 8.30pm.

By Tram or Bus

Trams are my favorite mode of transport. I especially enjoy touring the Ringstrasse by tram (numbers 1 and 2 go right round) to admire the fine architecture of the city center. As with buses, trams are identified by numbers and/or letters. Bus routes 1A, 2A, and 3A are city-center minihoppers. Most routes operate from 5am until midnight, when a useful network of night buses (marked with a blue 'N') operates until 5am. Details of individual routes can be found at www.wienerlinien.at.

By Taxi

There are taxi-ranks at many busy junctions, and outside most large hotels. You can hail a taxi in the street if its yellow sign is lit up, or book one by phone (☎ 01 601 60; 01 401 00; 01 313 00; 01 814 00).

By Car

Vienna's maze of narrow one-way streets, its expensive, restricted parking, and ubiquitous trams (which always take priority over other traffic) make driving in the city center decidedly stressful and best avoided. If you do drive anywhere in Austria, remember to keep to the right-hand side.

Fast **Facts**

APARTMENT RENTALS For long-term accommodation (including short-term lets), look at *Bazar* magazine, or online at www.bazar.at, for the latest listings of apartments or rooms to rent. The previous chapter (The Best Lodging) contains details of a couple of apartment-hotels.

ATMS The easiest way to get euros is via bank or credit card at one of the many ATMs (called *Bankomats*), which are dotted about the city. Be warned, however, you may be charged a fee for withdrawing money from your home bank account, and credit-card companies charge interest.

BABYSITTING Many mid- to upper-range hotels can arrange babysitting services. Otherwise, contact **WienXtra-Kinderinfo** (☎ 01 4000 84 400, www.kinderinfowien.at) for details of reputable babysitting agencies.

BANKING HOURS Most banks are open Monday through Friday from 9am to 3pm (4.30pm Thurs).

BIKE RENTALS Vienna has over 300km of marked cycle paths and plenty of bike-hire outlets (Mar–Oct), including **Pedal Power**, Ausstellungsstrasse 3 (☎ 01 729 7234, www.pedalpower.at); **Bicycle Rental Hochschaubahn**, Prater 113, by the roller-coaster ride (☎ 01 729 5858); and **Bicycle & Skate Rental Copa Cagrana**, Reichsbrücke, An Damm 1, Danube Island (☎ 01 263 5242, www.fahrradverleih.at). Prices start at around €5 (1 hour), €15 (half-day) and €24 (full day). There's also a bike-hire system called Citybike (Herrengasse 1-3, ☎ 0810 500 500, www.citybikewien.at), with over 50 pick-up points around town—look out for the distinctive circular red 'Citybike' sign. All you need is a credit card (MC or V) to release a bicycle at one of the bike stations. You can only hire one Citybike per card. The first hour is free of charge, then rates increase from €1 for 2 hours to €4 for 4 hours. You can return the Citybike to any bike station. The fee debited will depend on the time you return the bicycle to an empty bike box. If you don't have a credit card, you can buy a Tourist Card (€2 per day plus a small deposit) from Royal Tours, Herrengasse 1-3 (9am-11.30am; 1pm-6pm daily) or Pedal Power, Ausstellungsstrasse 3 (9am-7pm daily) and then pay the accrued fees when you return the card.

BUSINESS HOURS Most shops open Mon–Fri 9am–6pm (5pm Sat). Some larger stores open late on Thursdays

until 9pm. Supermarkets open Mon–Fri 8am–6pm or 7pm; until 5pm Sat. General office hours are Mon–Fri 8am–3.30pm (or sometimes 4 or 5pm).

CLIMATE See 'Weather'.

CONCERTS See 'Theater Tickets'.

CONSULATES & EMBASSIES American Embassy, Boltzmanngasse 16 (☎ 01 313 39–0, www.usembassy.at). **Canadian Embassy,** Laurenzerberg 2 (☎ 01 531 38 3000; www.kanada.at). **British Embassy,** Jauresgasse 12 (☎ 01 716 130; www.britishembassy.at). **Irish Embassy,** Rotenturmstrasse 16-18 (☎ 01 715 4246, www.embassyofireland.at). **Australian Embassy,** Mattiellistrasse 2 (☎ 01 506 740, www.australian-embassy.at). For other embassies and consulates, consult the Austrian Foreign Ministry website at www.bmaa.gv.at.

CUSTOMS Anyone arriving from outside the EU is allowed to bring into Austria up to 200 cigarettes, two bottles of wine, and one bottle of liquor, duty free. There are no limits for anyone arriving from another EU country. For specifics on what you can bring home with you, Americans should consult **US Customs** (☎ 202 354 1000, www.customs.gov). Canadians should contact the **Canadian Customs & Revenue Agency** (☎ 800 461 9999, www.ccra-adrc.gc.ca). British should contact **HM Revenue & Customs** (☎ 0845 010 9000, www.hmce.gov.uk). Australians should contact **Australian Customs Services** (☎ 02 6275 6666, www.customs.gov.au). New Zealanders should contact **New Zealand Customs** (☎ 1800 428 786 60, www.customs.govt.nz).

DENTISTS See 'Emergencies'.

DINING Breakfast in Vienna traditionally consists of a cup of coffee accompanied by a bread roll or croissant with butter, jam and sometimes a selection of cold cuts and cheeses. If your hotel doesn't include breakfast in its rates, it's the perfect excuse to indulge at one of the city's legendary coffee houses. Most cafés and coffee houses open from 7am to midnight, although some stay open later. Restaurants generally open 11am–3.30pm and 6pm–midnight. Some remain open all day. Dress codes are relaxed, except in a handful of more upmarket restaurants. Many restaurants require table reservations in advance, but they are generally not necessary in cafés, *Heurigen*, and less formal eateries. Ask your concierge to help with any arrangements on arrival in Vienna. Young children are welcome in most venues, with the exception of the more exclusive restaurants.

DOCTORS See 'Emergencies'.

ELECTRICITY Like most of Continental Europe, Austria uses the 220-volt system (two round prongs). American (110-volt) appliances will need both a transformer and an adapter plug. Some electronic items, including most laptops, have built-in transformers but will still need a simple adapter. UK 240-volt appliances need a continental adapter, widely available at home but difficult to find in Austria.

EMBASSIES See 'Consulates and Embassies'.

EMERGENCIES Dial 133 for **police**, 122 for **fire**, 144 for an **ambulance**, 141 for an **emergency doctor**. Hospitals (*Krankenhäuser*) with emergency facilities (open 24 hours a day, seven days a week) include: **Allgemeines Krankenhaus**, Währinger Gürtel (☎ 01 40400, www.akhwien.at); **Unfallkrankenhaus Meidling**, Kundratstrasse 37 (☎ 01 601 50–0, www.ukhmeidling.at); and **Lorenz Böhler Unfallkrankenhaus**, Donaueschingenstrasse 13 (☎ 01 33110, www.ukhboehler.at). A

dentists' emergency service operates after hours and at weekends on ☎ 01 512 2078. See also 'Pharmacies'.

EVENT LISTINGS The main listings magazine (German only) for what's on in the city is *Falter* (www.falter.at), published every Wednesday and available from kiosks and newsagents. The Tourist Office produces a monthly events listing covering theater, concerts, film festivals, spectator sports, exhibitions, and more, as well as a seasonal magazine, *Vienna Scene*. Look out also for the free monthly magazine *Enjoy Vienna* available in bars and hotels, and the Friday edition of the free newspaper *Heute* (in German) for further listings. Online, www.hauptstadt.at is a useful site to source information on nightlife, pop concerts, and cinema venues.

FAMILY TRAVEL Vienna is a surprisingly child-friendly city, with lots of attractions that appeal to youngsters. Look for the items tagged with a **kids** icon in this book. There's even a tourist office, WienXtra-Kinderinfo, devoted solely to kids (see Tourist Offices).

GAY & LESBIAN TRAVELERS The best gay and lesbian resources in Vienna are the Tourist Board's *Queer Guide*, and the *Gay Guide*, available in various bars and at the Tourist Info Wien office in Albertinaplatz. The **Rosa Lila Villa**, Linke Wienzeile 102 (www.villa.at) offers information, advice, and counseling in its Lesbian Center (☎ 01 586 8150) and the Gay Men's Center (☎ 01 585 4343).

HOLIDAYS Most shops and all banks and services are closed on public holidays, which are as follows: New Year's Day, Epiphany (Jan 6), Easter Sunday, Easter Monday, Labor Day (May 1), Ascension Day (6th Thurs after Easter), Whit Monday (6th Mon after Easter), Corpus Christi,

Assumption Day (Aug 15), National Holiday (Oct 26), All Saints Day (Nov 1), Feast of the Immaculate Conception (Dec 8), Christmas Day, and Stefanitag (Dec 26).

INSURANCE It is important to take out adequate personal travel insurance for your trip, covering medical expenses, theft, loss, repatriation, personal liability, and cancellation. Private medical insurance is essential for all non-EU visitors. However, thanks to a reciprocal agreement, citizens of the UK and other EU countries are entitled to reduced-price medical treatment on presentation of a valid European Health Insurance Card (EHIC—apply online at www.dh.gov.uk/travellers). Dental care, except emergency accident treatment, is not available free of charge and should also be covered by private medical insurance.

INTERNET CAFÉS Most Viennese hotels have Internet access in guest rooms, or an Internet terminal in the lobby. Many cafés offer the opportunity to log on to the Internet via Wi-Fi with your own wireless-enabled laptop. Internet cafés are scattered around town. A popular one is the **Netcafé** at the Künstlerhaus Kino, Karlsplatz 5 (corner of Academiestrasse, www.k-haus/at/kino/netcafe, daily 11am–9pm, €4 for 1 hour).

LOST PROPERTY Inform all credit-card companies immediately if your credit cards are stolen, and file a report at the local police station for any missing items if you intend to make an insurance claim. For help in finding lost property on a train, phone Südbahnhof (☎ 01 580 022 222); or on a tram or bus, phone the General Information Office (☎ 01 790 943 500). Otherwise, try the central lost property office, Zentrales Fundamt, Bastiengasse 36-38 (☎ 01 4000 8091; Mon–Fri 8am–3.30pm (until 5.30pm Thurs)).

MAIL & POSTAGE Austria's postal service is generally swift and reliable. Stamps (*Briefmarken*) can be bought at post offices, tobacconists, and some newspaper kiosks. Letter-boxes are plentiful and easy to find—they're bright yellow. Most post offices open Mon–Fri 8am–noon, 2pm–6pm. Some also open Sat 8am–noon. The post offices at Südbahnhof, Westbahnhof, and Franz-Josefs-Bahnhof open for longer hours (including Saturday and Sunday mornings), and the main post office at Fleischmarkt 19 (☎ 0577 677 1010, www.post.at) is open daily 6am–10pm.

MONEY Austria's currency is the euro, with notes issued in denominations of 5, 10, 20, 50, and 100 euros, and coins of 1 and 2 euros and also 1, 2, 10, 20, and 50 cents. Credit cards are widely used in Vienna (especially Visa and Master-Card) but it is a good idea to carry cash to use in bars and cafés, and to check the payment methods available before you order a meal or run up a bar bill. If you do get caught short, there are numerous bureaux de change around town, and most international banks' cash cards can be used to obtain cash in local currency from some ATMs, although the commission charged can be high. For up-to-date currency conversion information, go to www.xe.com.

ORIENTATION TOURS See 'Tours'.

PARKING In most streets within the Gürtel, you need a 30-, 60- or 90-minute *Parkschein* (parking ticket), available from tobacconists, banks, train stations, and Wiener Linien ticket offices. To validate it, cross out the appropriate time, date, and year and leave it visible on the dashboard. Parking restrictions are in force in the Innere Stadt from 9am–7pm (maximum 90min). If your car gets clamped for illegal parking, the fine for releasing it is €350. Car parks are marked with a blue P and charge around €2–€5 per hour. You'll find further information on parking in the Transportation section of www.wien.gv.at.

PASSES The **Vienna Card** (available from hotels and tourist offices, €18.50) provides 72 hours of unlimited travel by subway, bus, or tram plus 190 discounts at a variety of museums, attractions, cafés, restaurants, shops, and *Heurigen*. The card is available from the Tourist Info Wien office in Albertinaplatz, hotels, and all ticket offices of the Vienna Transport Authority. (High-school kids and students are already eligible for discounts at various Viennese sights with their international student card and so may not benefit from a Vienna Card.)

If you are planning to visit the Imperial Apartments, the Sisi Museum and silver collection at the Hofburg, Schönbrunn Palace and the Imperial furniture collection (20min from Schönbrunn at Andreasgasse 7, ☎ 01 524 3357–0, www.hofmobiliendepot.at, Tues–Sun 10am–6pm), you should invest in a **Sisi Ticket** (€22.50 adults, €11.50 kids aged 6–18, €46.90 family, valid for one year), making a saving of around 20% on the normal admission prices. It also means you don't have to wait if there are queues for any of the attractions—a big bonus during peak season.

PASSPORTS Citizens of the USA, Canada, the UK, Ireland, Australia and New Zealand need only a valid passport to enter Austria. Take a photocopy of your passport's information page and keep it somewhere separate. This will speed up the replacement process at your embassy if it gets lost or stolen. While in Vienna, keep your passport and other valuables in your room/hotel safe.

PHARMACIES Pharmacies (*Apotheken*) are recognizable by their red serpentine 'A'. Most open Mon–Fri 8am–6pm, Sat 8am–noon. After hours, there is a rota system. Either dial 1550 for information, or check at a local pharmacy—they all display a sign indicating the nearest one open.

SAFETY Crime rates are low in Vienna although it is advisable to take sensible precautions against petty crime: don't carry excess cash, and use the hotel safe for valuable goods; don't leave anything visible in a parked car; beware of pickpockets in crowded places (especially in the Naschmarkt); and stick to well-lit, populated areas by night. In particular, steer clear of parks after dusk (especially the Prater and the Stadtpark) and Karlsplatz underground station at night, which is a notorious drug-dealing hotspot. If you need a police station, ask for a *Polizeiwachzimmer*. For emergency police assistance, dial 133.

SENIOR TRAVELERS Discounts for seniors are available (with proof of age) for most museums, public transport, and entertainment.

SHOPPING See 'Business Hours'.

SMOKING The Viennese are big smokers and unlike many countries in the EU, at the time of publication the ban on smoking in public places has not yet come into force. There are some no-smoking (*Nichtraucher*) restaurants, and many others have no-smoking areas. Smoking is banned in all Austrian airports and railway stations.

SPECTATOR SPORTS The Austrians are football-crazy, especially having hosted the 2008 European Championships, with the national football league running from the fall until early spring. Two of the nation's top teams—Austria Memphis and Rapid—are based in Vienna. The main stadium is Ernst-Happel Stadium in the Prater, which seats nearly 50,000 (Meiereistrasse 7, ☎ 01 728 0854. U-Bahn 2 (Stadion)). Also in the Prater is the Freudenau race course (Rennbahnstrasse 65, ☎ 01 728 9531, www. freudenau.at, races Mar–Nov) and Krieau trotting arena (Nordportalstrasse 274, ☎ 01 728 0046, www.kreiau.at, races Sept–June). The Stadthalle (Vogelweidplatz 14, ☎ 01 981 000. www.stadthalle. com, U-Bahn 6 (Burggasse/Stadthalle)) hosts a variety of sporting events (and pop concerts), including ice hockey (Sept–Feb).

TAXES Visitors from non-EU countries are entitled to reclaim VAT (20%, called *Mehrwertsteuer*), which is included in the price of any purchase over €75. To claim, a tax-refund cheque must be filled out by the shop at the time of purchase (remember to take your passport). This is then stamped by border officials when you leave the EU. The refund is most easily claimed when leaving the country—there's a counter for instant refunds at Vienna International Airport, also one at Westbahnhof, Südbahnhof, and at major border crossings.

TAXIS See 'By Taxi', p 161.

TELEPHONES Austria's country code is ☎ 0043, **Vienna's** is ☎ 01. When calling a Viennese number from within the city, the local code is not required. Most public phone booths accept phone cards (available from post offices and newsagents) and coins. A minimum of €0.20 is needed to make a local call. Some post offices have phone booths where national and international calls can be made. Cheap rate calling is Mon–Fri 6pm–8am and at weekends. Avoid making international calls from your hotel as hefty surcharges are often added. For **directory enquiries** in Austria and the EU, dial 118877; for **international directory enquiries**, dial 0900 118877. International country codes for ringing home are as follows: **USA and Canada** ☎ 001; **UK** ☎ 0044; **Irish Republic** ☎ 00353; **Australia** ☎ 0061; and **New Zealand** ☎ 0064.

TICKETS See 'How to Get Tickets', p 138.

TIPPING There are no fixed rules for tipping, but a tip of around 10% is expected in taxis, and €1 per bag is normal for porters in hotels. Restaurant prices usually include a cover charge. If not, this has to be stated on the menu. It is customary to give a 10% tip or to round up the bill. Announce the total sum (including tip) to the waiter when they take your money. They will normally then pocket the tip and return your change.

TOILETS There are over 300 public toilets throughout the city (marked WC), mostly open 9am–7pm daily, although some are open 24 hours a day. Those with attendants cost around €0.50. At some stage, be sure to visit the beautiful Jugendstil toilets on Graben, which still retain their original 1905 green railings, lanterns marked Damen (for women) and Herren (for men), and brass washstands.

TOURIST OFFICES Vienna's main tourist office, **Tourist-Info Wien**, Albertinaplatz/corner of Maysedergasse (☎ 01 24555, www.vienna. info, daily 9am–7pm) provides maps, pamphlets, hotel bookings, souvenirs, and a ticket booking service. There's also a small tourist information office, **Tourist-Info Wien Airport**, in the airport Arrivals hall (☎ 01 7007 32875, daily 8.30am–9pm). **WienXtra Jugendinfo**, Babenbergerstrasse 1 (☎ 01 1799, www.jugendinfo wien.at, Mon–Sat noon–7pm) is an information service, aimed at visitors aged 14–26. It also sells reduced-rate tickets for various events and pop concerts. **WienXtra-Kinderinfo**, MuseumsQuartier (☎ 01 400 084 400, www.kinder infowien.at) is devoted solely to kids, with a small indoor playground and stacks of information on kids' activities.

TOURIST TRAPS Be careful not to be taken in by the sales pitches of the smooth-talking ticket touts dressed as Mozart look-alikes, who hang around the main tourist attractions waiting to pounce on unsuspecting visitors. The concert packages they offer tend to be touristy and over-priced. A couple of the more rep-utable establishments are listed in the Arts & Entertainment chapter, see p 133.

TOURS Vienna has several tour com-panies. **Cityrama**, Börsegasse 1 (☎ 01 534 13–0, www.cityrama.at) offers tours lasting from one hour (in central Vienna) and longer excur-sions to the Vienna Woods and nearby cities, including Salzburg, Prague, and Bratislava. An excellent way to explore the city is on the **Vienna Line** buses, Graf Starhem-berggasse 25 (☎ 01 712 4683-0, www.viennasightseeingtours.com). Buy a ticket for one hour (€13), 2 hours (€16), or 24 hours (€20) then hop on and off at the main sights as many times as you want between 10am and 8pm (buses run every 15–20 minutes, June–Aug, less fre-quently out of season). For some-thing a little different, I recommend a nostalgic hour-long tour in a vin-tage open-top coach with **Oldtimer Bus Tours**, Siedengasse 32 (☎ 01 503 744 312, www.oldtimertours.at, departing Heldenplatz daily 11am, 12.30pm, 2pm and 4pm, adults €18, kids €10) or, for the energetic, a 3-hour **City Segway Tour** (☎ 01 729 7234, www.citySegwayTours. com, departing 2pm daily from the Staatsoper; €70 per person, must be at least 12 years old). **Pedal Power**, Ausstellungsstrasse 3 (☎ 01 729 7234, www.pedalpower.at) offers two guided bike tours, each 2 1/2–3 hours long, taking in many of city's historic sights. For boat tours, see 'Danube Boat Trips', p 99.

TRAVELERS WITH DISABILITIES Vienna caters reasonably well for travelers with disabilities (*Behinderte*), although some of the older muse-ums and attractions have limited facilities. Most museums have ramps, and many U-Bahn stations have wheelchair lifts, but buses and older trams don't. The newer trams have doors at ground level. A plan of U-Bahn stations for sight-impaired visitors is available from **Wiener Lin-ien** (see p 158). The tourist office website (www.vienna.info) has excel-lent advice and detailed information on suitable hotels, restaurants, and attractions with disabled facilities, together with parking information, toilet locations, and much more in their 'Specials' section.

VAT See 'Taxes' above.

WEATHER See 'Climate'.

Vienna: **A Brief History**

c2000BC   First Indo-Germanic tribes settle in the region.

c400BC   Celtic tribes create a settle-ment called Vindebona at Hoher Markt.

15BC   Roman legions occupy Vin-debona. A further settlement (in today's Belvedere district) becomes a Roman garrison town.

c280 The Romans introduce viti-culture to the region.

433 Vindebona is destroyed by Huns, leading to a period of invasions by Goths, Avars, and Slav tribes.

8TH CENTURY Charlemagne deposes the Duke of Bavaria and founds the Carolingian Empire. First mention (in the Salzburg Annals) of the name 'Wenia' on the borders of the Eastern March or *Ostmark* (later renamed Ostarrichi).

976 The Babenbergs become margraves of the Eastern March.

1137 Vienna receives its town charter; construction of the Stephansdom begins.

1200 The city walls are erected.

1246 The last of the Babenbergs, Duke Frederick II, is killed. Control of Austria passes to King Otokar of Bohemia.

1278 Otokar is killed in the Battle of the Marchfeld against King Rudolf I von Habsburg. This marks the start of the Habsburg dynasty (which rules until 1918).

LATE MIDDLE AGES The Habsburg court becomes a cultural hub of central Europe, attracting numerous musicians and minstrels.

1365 Vienna University is founded.

1349 The Plague almost wipes out the entire population of Vienna.

15TH CENTURY A period of political and economic instability follows the massacre and expulsion of the Jews in 1421. After the Hussite Wars, Vienna temporarily falls under Hungarian rule.

1438 Albrecht V is elected Holy Roman Emperor and Vienna becomes the seat of the Empire.

1469 Vienna is made a bishopric and the Stephansdom becomes a cathedral.

1493 Emperor Maximilian I drives the Hungarians out of Austria.

1498 Maximilian I founds the Vienna Boys' Choir.

1521 Ferdinand I becomes sovereign of Lower Austria and abolishes Vienna's special privileges. The citizens revolt and Ferdinand responds with violent suppression. Following the King of Hungary's death, Ferdinand I lays claim to the Hungarian crown and attempts to expand his authority throughout the region. In reaction, the Sultan of the Ottoman Empire declares war on the Habsburgs.

1529 The first Turkish siege takes place. After the withdrawal of the Turks, Vienna is transformed into a fortress to protect it from continued Ottoman threat.

1571 Following the Reformation, Protestant Maximilian II allows religious freedom. At this time, 8% of the city is Protestant.

1618–48 A Bohemian rebellion starts the Thirty Years' War. In 1623 the Counter-Reformation begins.

1629 A further plague claims 30,000 lives.

1638 The Turks invade again, bringing with them a lasting 'gift'—bags of coffee.

1683–1736 Prince Eugène of Savoy leads the Imperial Army to victory against the Turks and the French, and reasserts the Habsburg Empire's status as a major power. Vienna becomes an international center of arts and music.

1740 Maria Theresa—the greatest of all Habsburg rulers—ascends the throne. Her 40-year reign ushers in a golden era.

18TH CENTURY Vienna develops from a court-based feudal society into the dazzling bourgeois capital of a great European power. The death penalty is abolished and there is greater tolerance towards Jews and non-Catholic Christians. Majestic palaces, churches, summer residences, and parks spring up throughout the city.

1750–1830 Music flourishes in Vienna. Gluck, Haydn, Mozart, Beethoven, and Schubert all live and work in the city.

1792 The reign of Franz II begins. He is later appointed Holy Roman Emperor.

1805 Napoleon lays siege to Vienna; Franz II gives up the title of Holy Roman Emperor in 1806, becoming Franz I of Austria.

1809 Napoleon invades again and takes up residence in the Schönbrunn Palace. In 1810 he marries Franz I's daughter, Archduchess Marie Louise.

EARLY 19TH CENTURY The onset of industrialization leads to a rapid increase in Vienna's population.

1825 Johann Strauss forms his first waltz orchestra, and his two sons, Johann and Josef, follow in his footsteps.

1848 The citizens rise up against political repression. Ferdinand I abdicates in favor of his nephew, Franz Josef.

1848–1916 Franz Josef transforms Vienna into a magnificent modern metropolis. The Ringstrasse becomes a grand boulevard with elegant public buildings.

1867 Franz Josef becomes the dual monarch of Austria-Hungary.

1869 The State Opera House opens with a performance of Mozart's *Don Giovanni* on May 25.

1897 The association of artists known as the 'Secession' is founded, led by Gustav Klimt.

1897–1910 New mass political parties start to emerge, including German Nationalism and the Social Democrats. Anti-Semite Karl Lueger, leader of the Christian Socialist Party, becomes Vienna's mayor.

1903 The Wiener Werkstätte is founded.

1914 Archduke Franz Ferdinand is assassinated in Sarajevo, starting the chain-reaction slide towards World War I.

1918 World War I ends, the dual monarchy collapses and Austria becomes a republic on November 12.

1920–34 Socialism prevails in so-called 'Red Vienna'.

1938 Anschluss: Hitler annexes his home country, and Austria becomes his 'Ostmark' in the Third German Reich.

1945 World War II ends. The Russians occupy Vienna on April 11, followed by the other Allies.

1955 A treaty signed in the Belvedere Palace marks the end of the Allied occupation and guarantees Austria's sovereignty and neutrality.

1979 With the building of the International Center, Vienna becomes the third United Nations city, after New York and Geneva.

1995 Austria joins the EU and the Eurozone.

2006 Austria assumes presidency of the EU.

2008 Vienna hosts the 2008 European Football Championships.

2009 Vienna celebrates the 200th anniversary of Haydn's death.

Vienna's **Art & Architecture**

Few cities can match Vienna's architectural riches. Indeed, the entire city center has been declared a UNESCO World Cultural Heritage Site due to the remarkable diversity and quality of its buildings.

Early Architecture
Little survives of Vienna's earliest architecture except some Roman remains at **Michaelerplatz** and in the **Römermuseum** in Hoher Markt. Few buildings retain any Romanesque features either. The rounded arches, thick walls, and small windows typical of this period were mostly replaced by the medieval Gothic style in the 13th century. The finest example is the city's oldest church—the **Ruprechtskirche**.

Gothic: 1150–1550
The Gothic style imported from France enabled builders to make walls thinner and taller, with large windows to let in more natural light. Other Gothic features included pointed arches, delicate stonework tracery, flying buttresses (free-standing exterior pillars to support the building), and elaborately constructed ceilings, using the newly acquired techniques of cross-vaulting and fan-vaulting.

The intricate filigree work of the **Maria am Gestade Church** and the soaring proportions of the magnificent **Stephansdom** are both textbook examples of the Gothic style.

Renaissance: 1550–1650
The Renaissance style was first developed in Florence, Italy, as a conscious revival of certain aspects of ancient Greek and Roman design, with an emphasis on geometry and regularity, enlivened by decoration.

Symmetry, proportion, and the use of a classical 'vocabulary' of columns, lintels, arches, domes, and niches are the main characteristics of this architectural style.

Surprisingly few Renaissance buildings survive in Vienna. The city was frequently under attack during this period, so precious resources of building materials were used to strengthen the fortifications. Fine examples include the **Stallburg**, the **Schweizertor**, and the striking gabled façade of the **Franziskanerkirche** (the interior is a mishmash of Gothic, Renaissance, and baroque styles).

Baroque & Rococo: 1650–1800
Vienna is best known for the splendor of its baroque palaces and churches. This was Vienna's golden age, and baroque became the favored style of the Habsburgs who, finally freed from the financial burdens of repeated wars and invasions, embarked on an unprecedented building spree. Originating in Italy, the baroque style modified the classical ground-rules of Renaissance architecture, using them in a more theatrical way, which appealed to the emotions. Running in tandem with the Counter-Reformation, the baroque style also clearly underlined the wealth and power of the Catholic Church and the Habsburg rulers. Key features of baroque include classical forms enhanced by grand curving lines, exuberant ornamentation and carving (often in gilt, stucco, or marble), monumental ceiling frescoes, a

dramatic use of color, light and shade, plus illusory effects like *trompe l'oeil*.

The rococo style developed in the early 18th century as an even more ornate, blousey version of baroque, involving vast quantities of gilded stucco and brightly colored frescoes. This was the favorite style of the Empress Maria Theresa, hence Austrian rococo is sometimes referred to as 'late-baroque Theresian style'.

Karlskirche is the crown jewel of Vienna's baroque treasures, designed by the Austrian architect Fischer von Erlach, who also built the **Schönbrunn Palace** and the **Prunksaal**—Austria's finest example of secular baroque—in the Nationalbibliothek. The **Belvedere Palace**, **Schwarzenberg Palace**, and **St. Peter's Church**—all impressive baroque edifices—were created by his successor, Lukas von Hildebrandt. To see the finest rococo interiors in the city, visit the **Schönbrunn Palace** and the **Academy of Sciences**.

Biedermeier: 1815–1850
A new bourgeois culture known as Viennese 'Biedermeier' emerged after the Napoleonic Wars and the Congress of Vienna in 1815. This left its mark not only on architecture, but also on interior design and the visual arts, paving the way for the later styles known as Jugendstil (Art Nouveau) and the Secession. The main characteristics of the Biedermeier style are simplicity, elegance, and functionality of design.

Splendid examples of Viennese Biedermeier architecture include the **Stadttempel** and the **Dreimäderlhaus**.

Historicism (Neoclassicism): 1800–1880
At the peak of his power following the 1848 Revolution, the young

Emperor Franz Josef I set about upstaging Napoleon III's radical makeover of Paris. He invited the most famous architects in Europe to create a magnificent new boulevard right round the heart of Vienna's historic city center, or Innere Stadt. Known as the Ringstrasse, it became a showcase for bombastic imperial buildings, which lined it on either side. The fashionable style at that time was a version of neoclassicism known in Vienna as 'Historicism'. This was a reaction against the fussy complexities of baroque and rococo architecture, and a reversion to the purer classicism of yesteryear. Historicism was characterized by clean, elegant lines, balance and symmetry, and the use of neoclassical motifs and columns.

Typical examples of Viennese Historicism on the Ringstrasse include the **Burgtheater**, the **Kunsthistorisches Museum (KHM)** and the **Naturhistorisches Museum (NHM)** epitomizing the Italian neo-Renaissance style. The **Parliament Building** evokes a Greek interpretation of Historicism with its columns and statues of Greek philosophers. Also along the Ringstrasse are several fine neo-Gothic edifices, including the **Votivkirche** and **Neues Rathaus**.

Jugendstil & Secession: 1880–1920
The collision of tradition and modernity in Vienna around 1900 created an unusually fertile climate for the arts. Architects felt constrained by neoclassicism, although they found the clean lines and elegant styles appealing. As the Art Nouveau movement emerged in other parts of Europe, Vienna spawned its own distinctive version, known as Jugendstil (Young Style). Classic hallmarks of the style include simple, functional lines; organic, flowing motifs (often flowers, flames, waves

or flowing hair); extensive use of iron, stucco, and stained glass.

In 1897, an iconoclastic splinter-group called the Secession was formed, led by Klimt, Wagner, Olbrich, and Hoffman. This uniquely Viennese style stripped away some of the more decorative aspects of Jugendstil, focusing more on functionalism and geometry.

The best examples of the style in Vienna include the iconic **Secession Building**, Wagner's **Pavilions**, the **Postsparkasse**, **Majolika Haus**, and Loos' **American Bar**.

Modern Architecture: 1970–

The post-war years marked a lean architectural period in Vienna as Austria struggled to cope with the ignominy of military defeat and economic recession. However, during the early 1970s and 80s a new generation of architects emerged to create some highly imaginative structures. Pre-eminent among them was the eccentric genius, Friedensreich Hundertwasser, whose multicolored **KunstHausWien**, **Hundertwasser-haus**, and **Fernwärme** incinerator brighten the modern cityscape. Hundertwasser died at the turn of the millennium, but this creative trend has continued into the 21st century. No single style predominates, but the use of glass and steel is widespread. The innovative **Gasometer** development and Hans Hollein's hugely controversial **Haas Haus**, right at the heart of the UNESCO-protected Innere Stadt (city center), are noteworthy examples of the quirky modern style.

Useful Words & Phrases

ENGLISH	GERMAN	PRONUNCIATION
Good day	Guten Tag	goo-ten tag
How are you?	Wie geht es Ihnen?	vee gait es ee-nen
very well	Sehr gut	zair goot
thank you	Danke	dan-ke
you're welcome	Bitte sehr	bi-te zair
goodbye	Auf Wiedersehen	owf vee-der-zain
please	Bitte	bi-te
yes/no	Ja/Nein	yah/niyn
excuse me/sorry	Entschuldigung	ent-shool-di-gung
Where is/are . . . ?	Wo is/sind . . . ?	Voh ist/zint
left/right	links/rechts	links/rekhts
straight on	geradeaus	ge-raa-de-ows
I would like...	Ich hätte gerne...	Ick he-te ger-ne
Do you have a . . . ?	Haben Sie ein . . . ?	Hah-ben zee eyn
How much is it?	Wie viel kostet es?	Vee feel kos-tet es
When?	Wann?	Van
What?	Was?	Vas
yesterday	Gestern	ges-tern
today	Heute	hoi-te
tomorrow	Morgen	mor-gen
good/bad	gut/schlecht	goot/shlekt
better	besser	be-ser
more/less	mehr/weniger	mair/vay-niger
Do you speak English?	Sprechen Sie Englisch?	Shpre-khen zee eng-lish

ENGLISH	GERMAN	PRONUNCIATION
I don't understand	**Ich verstehe nicht**	*ich fer-shtaia nikht*
The bill please	**die Rechnung bitte**	*die rekh-nung bi-te*
I'm looking for . . .	**Ich suche . . .**	*ich zoo-khe*
the station	**der Bahnhof**	*dair baan-hof*
a hotel	**ein Hotel**	*eyn ho-tel*
the market	**der Markt**	*dair mahrkt*
a restaurant	**ein Restaurant**	*eyn res-tow-ron*
a toilet	**eine Toilette**	*ey-ne twa-le-te*
a bank	**eine Toilette**	*ey-ne bank*
a pharmacy	**eine Apotheke**	*ey-ne a-po-tay-ke*
a doctor	**ein Arzt**	*eyn artst*
breakfast	**Frühstück**	*froo-shtook*
lunch	**Mittagessen**	*mi-taak-essen*
dinner	**Abendessen**	*ar-bend-essen*
coffee and cake	**Kaffee und Kuchen**	*ka-fe unt koo-khen*
The menu please	**die Karte bitte**	*dee kaar-te bi-te*

Numbers

1	**ins**	*intz*
2	zwei	*tsvai*
3	**rei**	*drai*
4	vier	*feer*
5	**ünf**	*fuenf*
6	sechs	*zeks*
7	**sieben**	*zee-ben*
8	acht	*akht*
9	**neun**	*noin*
10	zehn	*tsen*

Days of the Week

Monday	**Montag**	*mawn-taag*
Tuesday	Dienstag	*deens-taag*
Wednesday	**Mittwoch**	*mit-vokh*
Thursday	Donnerstag	*do-ners-taag*
Friday	**Freitag**	*frai-taag*
Saturday	Samstag	*zams-taag*
Sunday	**Sonntag**	*zon-taag*

Index

See also Accommodations and Restaurant indexes, below.

Photo **Credits**